THE MORTIFICATION
OF SIN

THE TREASURES OF JOHN OWEN

THE MORTIFICATION OF SIN

Abridged and made easy to read by
Richard Rushing

THE BANNER OF TRUTH TRUST

THE BANNER OF TRUTH TRUST

Head Office
3 Murrayfield Road
Edinburgh
EH12 6EL
UK

North America Office
PO Box 621
Carlisle
PA 17013
USA

banneroftruth.org

First published 2004
© Richard Rushing 2004
Reprinted 2005, 2007, 2008, 2009,
2016, 2020

*

ISBN: 978 0 85151 867 1

*

Typeset in 10.5/14 Sabon
at The Banner of Truth Trust, Edinburgh

Printed in the USA by
Versa Press Inc.,
East Peoria, IL.

*

Except where stated, Scripture quotations are from
THE HOLY BIBLE, ENGLISH STANDARD VERSION
© 2001 by Crossway Bibles, a division of Good News Publishers

Contents

Preface

I will briefly acquaint you with the main reasons for my consenting to publish the following discourse.

1. *The present state of professing believers.*

My primary reason is the obvious difficulty that most professing Christians have in dealing with the temptations that surround them. These arise in large measure from the fact that at this time they are both at peace in the world and divided among themselves. So important is this issue to me that I will be pleased if all I can do by the present work is to encourage others to press on men's consciences the need to consider their ways, and to give believers clearer directions on how to proceed in the mortification of sin.

2. *Dangerous mistakes concerning mortification.*

My second main reason is the dangerous mistakes some have fallen into recently in dealing with this subject.

Through lack of acquaintance with the mystery of the gospel and the efficacy of the death of Christ, they have imposed a system of self-wrought mortification on the necks of their disciples which neither they nor their fore-fathers were ever able to bear. The mortification they press is not suitable to the gospel in nature or effect, and regularly has the deplorable outcome of producing super-stition, self-righteousness and anxiety of conscience in those who take their teaching up.

What I here present, though in weakness, I humbly hope will answer to the spirit and letter of the gospel, as well as to the experience of those who know what it is to walk with God, according to the tenor of the covenant of grace. Certainly, something of this kind is needed now to promote the work of gospel mortification in the hearts of believers and direct them into safe paths where they will find rest for their souls.

Having preached on this subject, with some success, through the grace of Him who ministers seed to the sower, I was encouraged by friends in whose hearts are the ways of God to publish what I had delivered. I could not help recalling the debt I already stood under through promising to provide a treatise on *Communion with God*.[1] I thought that, if I could not yet settle the larger

---

[1] See Owen's *Works*, vol. 2 (London: Banner of Truth, 1967), 'On Communion with God', pp. 1–274; and *Communion with God* (Edinburgh: Banner of Truth, 1991) in the present series of abridgements which seek to make 'the treasures of John Owen' more accessible to present-day readers.

debt, I might at least offer them this discourse on *fighting against themselves* as an interest payment, in return for their forbearance, while they wait for the discourse on *peace and communion with God.*

Besides, I thought that, having been providentially engaged in public debate on various controversies in religion, I might provide something of more general use, as a matter of choice, rather than of necessity.

For these and similar reasons I have brought this short discourse to public view, and now present it to you. I hope I may truly claim that my heart's desire to God and my main aim in the station in which the good providence of God has placed me is that mortification and universal holiness may be promoted in my heart and in the hearts and lives of others, to the glory of God; and that in this way the gospel of our Lord and Saviour Jesus Christ may be adorned in all things. If this little discourse may be in any way useful to this end to the least of the saints, I will look on this as an answer to the weak prayers with which it is attended, by its unworthy author,

JOHN OWEN
Oxford
1656

Publisher's Foreword

Among the writers of the Puritan era of the seventeenth century, none has been more highly regarded than John Owen. His works combine biblical insight and theology with spirituality and experiential religion to a very marked degree. The value that the present publishers place on him is seen in the fact that the sixteen volumes of his *Works* (in the Goold edition of 1850–3) have been kept continuously in print ever since they were first reprinted in 1965–8, and the seven volumes of his exposition of *Hebrews* have been available since 1991.

The present series of abridgements is not intended to replace the full text, which we hope to keep in print, but to make the treasures contained in Owen's writings more accessible to present-day readers. The books already published in this series, abridged by Dr R. J. K. Law, have been well received. The most recent, *The Spirit and the Church*, was welcomed by one reviewer as 'another skilled abridgement (with sensitive modernising of language) of John Owen by evangelical clergyman Dr Law. The outstanding Puritan is brought wholly within reach of everyone, yet without any damage to the sense . . . We would urge readers to try this as an introduction to the ministry of John Owen. Dr Law has made the great man easy, so that today's reader may enjoy the large variety of topics – many of them being the very questions which pastors never seem to answer. You really would not realise you were reading a Puritan – except for the freshness and helpfulness of the material.'[1]

The present work has been abridged and paraphrased by Richard Rushing, the minister of Bethany Baptist Church, Martinez, California,[2] from volume 6 of Owen's *Works*. Originally entitled *Of the Mortification of Sin in Believers; the Necessity, Nature and Means of It*, it is essentially an exposition and application of Romans 8:13. Owen deals with a topic seldom expounded today, the need for Christians to engage in a life-long struggle, through faith in Christ and by the power of the Spirit, against the sinful and corrupt tendencies which continue to work in them till the day they die. The subject may be particularly helpful in a day not unlike Owen's (as he characterizes it in his Preface) when believers, at least in the West, are generally at peace in the world and divided among themselves. The peculiar temptations of such a time are obvious on every hand. The remedy for them is the same as it has always been.

THE PUBLISHER
January 2004

[1] Metropolitan Tabernacle Bookshop, Autumn 2002.
[2] We hope to continue to publish Owen abridgements, both by Dr Law and occasionally by other writers. For details of the series, see the notes at the end of this book.

1

Introduction

If by the Spirit you put to death the deeds of the body,
you will live (Rom. 8:13)

This is the main text and foundation upon which this discourse is based. In this text we find:

1. *To whom it is directed:* 'You believers.'
2. *The condition:* 'If you.'
3. *The means of accomplishment:* 'The Spirit.'
4. *A duty:* 'Put to death the deeds of the body.'
5. *A promise:* 'You will live.'

1. *The exhortation is directed toward believers.*
Paul is speaking to believers in that he says in verse 1 of the same chapter, 'There is therefore now no condemnation' to them. In verse 9 he explains, 'You are not in

the flesh but in the Spirit,' and in verses 10 and 11 he speaks to those who are quickened by the Spirit of Christ.

The persons to whom this duty is directed, and the duty itself, are the foundation of this book. It is expressed in this thesis:

The choicest believers, who are assuredly freed from the condemning power of sin, should also make it their business all of their days to mortify the indwelling power of sin.

2. *The condition expresses the certainty of the relationship.*

The purpose of the condition, 'If you', is to express the certainty of the relationship between the cure and the result. There is a clear connection between the mortifying of the deeds of the body and living. This connection is not cause and effect properly and strictly, for 'eternal life is the gift of God through Jesus Christ' (*Rom.* 6:23), but rather means and end. The intent of the text in this conditional expression is that there is a certain infallible connection and coherence between true mortification and eternal life: if you use this means, you shall obtain that end; if you do mortify, you shall live. This then, is our main motive for the enforcement of this duty in our lives.

3. *Our strength in the performance of this duty comes through the Spirit.*

All other ways of mortification are in vain. Men may attempt this work based upon other principles, but they will come short. It is a work of the Spirit, and it is by Him alone that we are to experience victory. Mortification from a self-strength, carried on by ways of self-invention, to the end of a self-righteousness, is the soul and substance of all false religion in the world.

4. *The duty itself.*

Let us consider three things concerning the duty before us: i. What is meant by 'the body'; ii. What is meant by 'the deeds of the body'; and iii. What is meant by mortifying or putting them to death.

i. 'The body', at the end of the verse, is the same as 'the flesh' in the beginning of the verse. It is indwelling sin, the corrupted flesh or lust, that is intended.

ii. The outward 'deeds' of the body are here expressed, yet the inward cause is chiefly intended. The apostle calls them 'deeds' in that they are an outward expression of a yielding to an inward lust. Indwelling lust and sin is the fountain and principle of all sinful action.

iii. To 'mortify' means to put any living thing to death. To kill a man, or any other living thing, is to take away the principle of all its strength, vigour, and power, so that it cannot act, or exert, or put forth any proper actings of its own. Indwelling sin is compared to a person, a living person, called 'the old man', with his faculties, and properties, his wisdom, craft, subtlety, and strength. The 'old man' is utterly mortified and slain by the cross of Christ. He is said to be 'crucified with Christ' (*Rom.* 6:6), and ourselves to be 'dead' with him, verse 8. This takes place in regeneration. The work of the Holy Spirit, Who is planted in our hearts, also opposes the lusts of the flesh (*Gal.* 5:17). This whole work is done by degrees, and is to be carried on towards perfection all of our days.

Thus it is the constant duty of believers to render a death blow to the deeds of the flesh, that they may not have life and strength to bring forth their destructive influence.

5. *The promise is life.*

The life promised is eternal life. This is the very opposite of the penalty: 'If you live after the flesh, you shall die.' However, the word may not only mean eternal life in heaven, but also the spiritual life in Christ which we have here, the joy and comfort and vigour of our life yet in this world.

This is a second motive for the duty prescribed: the vigour, power, and comfort of our spiritual life depend on the mortification of the deeds of the flesh.

2

Why the Flesh Must Be Mortified

P aul, in speaking to believers, thus challenges the Colossians: 'Mortify therefore your members which are upon the earth' (*Col.* 3:5, AV). Do you mortify? Do you make it your daily work? You must always be at it while you live; do not take a day off from this work; always be killing sin or it will be killing you.

Your position in Christ, and the new life that you have in Him, does not excuse you from this work. Our Saviour tells us how His Father deals with every branch in Him that beareth fruit; every true and living branch, 'He prunes [it], that it may bear more fruit' (*John* 15:2). He prunes it, and not just for a day or two, but as long as it is a branch in this world. Paul describes his practice: 'I discipline my body and keep it under control' (*1 Cor.* 9:27). This was his daily business. If this was the work and business of Paul, who was so exalted in grace, revelations, enjoyments, privileges, and consolations above the ordinary measure of believers, how can we be exempt from this work and duty while we are in the world?

Let us consider six reasons for our need to be at this important work.

1. *Indwelling sin always abides while we are in this world;* therefore, there is always a need for it to be mortified.

Some have wrongly and foolishly believed that we are able in this life to keep the commands of God perfectly and are wholly and perfectly dead to sin. Through ignorance of the true life in Christ and His power in believers, they have invented a new righteousness that is not in the gospel. They are vainly puffed up by their fleshly minds. Indwelling sin continues to live in believers in some measure and degree while we are in this world. We should not speak as though we had already attained, or were already perfect (*Phil.* 3:12). Our 'inner nature is being renewed day by day' while we live (2 *Cor.* 4:16); and according to the renovations of the new are the breaches and decays of the old. While we are here we 'know in part' (1 *Cor.* 13:12). There is a remaining darkness to be gradually removed by our growth in the knowledge of our Lord Jesus Christ (2 *Pet.* 3:18); and 'the flesh lusteth against the Spirit, so that we cannot do the things that we would' (*Gal.* 5:17, AV). We are therefore defective in our obedience as well as in our light (1 *John* 1:8). We have a 'body of death' (*Rom.* 7:24); from which we are not delivered but by the death of our bodies (*Phil.* 3:21). It is our duty to mortify, to be killing the sin while it is in us. We must be at this work. He that is appointed to kill an enemy, has only done half his work if he quits before the enemy is dead (*Gal.* 6:9; *Heb.* 12:1; *2 Cor.* 7:1).

2. *Sin is still acting and labouring to bring forth the deeds of the flesh.*

When sin lets us alone, we may let sin alone; but sin is always active when it seems to be the most quiet, and its waters are often deep when they are calm. We should therefore fight against it and be vigorous at all times and in all conditions, even when there is the least suspicion. 'The flesh lusteth against the Spirit' (*Gal.* 5:17, AV); lust is still tempting to and conceiving sin (*James* 1:14). It is called 'sin which clings so closely' (*Heb.* 12:1). Sin is always acting, always conceiving, and always seducing and tempting. Who can say that he has ever had anything to do with God or for God which indwelling sin has not tried to corrupt? This battle will last more or less all our days. If sin is always acting, we are in trouble if we are not always mortifying. He that stands still and allows his enemies to exert double blows upon him without resistance will undoubtedly be conquered in the end. If sin is subtle, watchful, strong, and always at work in the business of killing our souls, and we are slothful, negligent, and foolish in this battle, can we expect a favourable outcome? There is not a day but sin foils or is foiled, prevails or is prevailed upon. It will always be so while we live in this world. Sin will not spare for one day. There is no safety but in a constant warfare for those who desire deliverance from sin's perplexing rebellion.

3. *Sin, if not continually mortified, will bring forth great, cursed, scandalous, and soul-destroying sins* (*Gal.* 5:19–20).

You know what sin did in David, and in others. Every time sin rises to tempt or entice, it always seeks to express itself in the extreme. Every unclean thought or glance would be adultery if it could; every covetous desire would be oppression; and every unbelieving thought would be atheism. It is like the grave that is never satisfied.

In this we see the deceitfulness of sin. It gradually prevails to harden man's heart to his ruin (*Heb.* 3:13). Sin's expression is modest in the beginning but, once it has gained a foothold, it continues to take further ground and presses on to greater heights. This advance of sin keeps the soul from seeing that it is drifting from God. The soul becomes indifferent to the seed of sin as it continues to grow. This growth has no boundaries but utter denial of God and opposition to Him. Sin precedes higher by degrees; it hardens the heart as it advances. This enables the deceitfulness of sin to drive the soul deeper and deeper into sin. Nothing can prevent this but mortification. Mortification withers the root and strikes at the head of sin every hour. The best saints in the world are in danger of a fall if found negligent in this important duty!

4. *The Holy Spirit and our new nature are given to us to oppose sin and lust* (*Gal.* 5:17; 2 *Pet.* 1:4). It is our participation in the divine nature that gives us an escape from the pollutions that are in the world through lust. We need to employ the Holy Spirit and our new nature in this battle for our souls. If we neglect to make use of what we have received, God may justly hold His hand from giving us more. His graces and gifts are bestowed on us to use, exercise, and get benefit from. If we do not seek daily to mortify sin, we sin against the goodness, kindness, wisdom, grace, and love of God, Who has given us the weapons of our warfare.

5. *Neglect of this duty makes the inner man decay instead of renewing him.* Paul affirms (2 *Cor.* 4:16) that the inward man is renewed day by day, while the outward man perishes. Those who neglect mortification allow the inner man to perish. Grace in the heart must have exercise. If it is allowed to lie still, it withers and decays (*Rev.* 3:2), and sin seeks to harden our hearts (*Heb.* 3:13). The omission of mortification withers grace while lust flourishes. The frame of the heart grows worse and worse. When sin gains a considerable victory, it breaks the bones of the soul (*Psa.* 31:10; 51:8). It makes a man weak, sick, and ready to die (*Psa.* 38:3–5), so that he cannot look up (*Psa.* 40:12).

When poor creatures will take blow after blow, wound after wound, foil after foil, and never rise up to a vigorous opposition, can they expect any thing but to be hardened through the deceitfulness of sin, and that their souls should bleed to death (*2 John* 8)? It is a sad thing to consider the fearful outcome of this neglect, which threatens us each day. Do we not see broken hearted Christians, who were humble, tender, fearful to offend, and zealous for God in all His ways, turn earthly, carnal, cold, and wrathful through a neglect of this duty? They learn to comply with the men of the world and the things of the world to the scandal of their faith.

Today, true mortification is all but lost between the rigid, stubborn frame of spirit which is earthly, legal, harsh, critical, consistent with wrath, envy, malice and pride, on the one hand, and pretences of liberty, grace, and I know not what, on the other.

6. *Our spiritual growth is our daily duty*. It is our duty to be 'perfecting holiness in the fear of God' (*2 Cor.* 7:1, AV), to be 'growing in grace' every day (*1 Pet.* 2:2; *2 Pet.* 3:18), so that our inner nature should be renewed day by day (*2 Cor.* 4:16). This cannot be accomplished without the daily mortifying of sin. Sin sets its strength against every act of holiness, and every degree of spiritual growth. We will not be making progress in holiness without walking over the bellies of our lusts. He who does not kill sin along the way is making no progress in his journey.

The main point thus far: Even while we claim the meritorious mortification of our sin through the work of the cross of Christ, and though the implantation of our new life in Christ is in opposition to and destructive of the expression of sin, sin remains, acts, and works in the best of believers while we are yet in this world. It must be our constant daily duty to mortify it.

Before proceeding, I cannot but note that even though there is in this generation a growing number of professors, a great noise of religion, religious duties in every corner, and preaching in abundance, there is little evidence of the fruit of true mortification. Perhaps we might find that, judging by the principle of mortification, the number of true believers is not as multiplied as it appears from those who have made a mere profession. Some speak and profess a spirituality that far exceeds the former days, but their lives give evidence of a miserable unmortified heart. If vain spending of time, idleness, envy, strife, variance, emulations, wrath, pride, worldliness, selfishness (*1 Cor.* 1), are the mark of Christians, we have them among us in abundance. May the good Lord send us a spirit of mortification to cure our distempers, or we will be in a sad condition!

There are two evils which certainly accompany every unmortified professor, the first, in himself, and the second, with respect to others.

First, in himself. The basic characteristic of an unmortified course is the digestion of sin without bitterness in the heart. He who is able to swallow and digest daily sins in his life without conviction in the heart is at the very brink of turning the grace of God into lasciviousness, and being hardened by the deceitfulness of sin.

Let a man pretend what he will, little concern over sin is a serious offence to the grace and mercy of God!

There is no greater evidence of a false and rotten heart in the world than to deal in such a trade. To claim the blood of Christ, which is given to cleanse us (*1 John* 1:7; *Titus* 2:14); the exaltation of Christ, which is to give us repentance (*Acts* 5:31); the doctrine of grace, which teaches us to deny all ungodliness (*Titus* 2:11-12); and then to allow sin, is a rebellion that in the outcome will break the bones. From this door have gone out from us most of the professors that have apostatized in the days in which we live. For a while most of them were under conviction, and they 'escaped the defilements of the world through the knowledge of our Lord and Saviour Jesus Christ' (*2 Pet.* 2:20). But after having become acquainted with the doctrines of the gospel, they became weary of their spiritual duties. They had no true desire for these, and they allowed evil instead to lay hold of them, and speedily tumble them into perdition.

Second, to others. Unmortified professors have an evil influence on others in two ways:

i. Others are hardened in their own sin by persuading themselves that they are in just as good a condition as the unmortified professor. They see their zeal for religion, but it is not accompanied with righteousness. They view their worldly and selfish lives. They see them talk spiritually but live vainly. They hear them mention communion with God, and yet they are in every way conformed to the world. They see them boast of forgiveness of sins, and yet never forgive others. Thus, as they see the stain of sin in the unmortified professor, they harden their own hearts in their unregeneracy.

ii. It deceives them to think that if they can just be as good as the unmortified professor it shall be well with them. In reality they might even go farther in 'holiness' than the unmortified professor, and yet still fall short of eternal life.

3

The Work of the Spirit
in Mortification

The Holy Spirit is our only sufficiency for the work of mortification. All ways and means apart from Him have no true effect. He only is the great power behind it, and He works in us as He pleases.

1. *Vain methods of mortification.*

In vain do men seek other remedies that are not able to heal them. Many ways have been suggested to accomplish mortification. The greatest part of popish religion consists in mistaken ways and means to this end. They arouse the conviction of sin, but use poison as their cure. This can never deliver them from the anguish of conviction. Their vows, orders, fastings, penances, and rough garments all have the goal of mortification, but they seek to mortify dead creatures. They themselves are ignorant of the true nature and work of mortification. What they glory in is to their shame.

Many who have more light and knowledge of the gospel also insist on and prescribe the same false teachings about mortification. They have their outside endeavours, bodily exercises, self-performances, and mere legal duties without the least mention of Christ or His Spirit. In their swelling words of vanity they pass over the only means for the true mortification of sin. They show their deep-rooted blindness to the power of God and the mystery of the gospel. This is one of the important reasons for the publication of this discourse.

Why cannot these actions truly mortify one sin?

i. Many of the ways and means used were never appointed by God for this purpose. There is no power attained from these means unless God has appointed them for this very purpose. As to their rough garments, their vows, penances, disciplines, their course of monastic life, and the like; concerning all these God will say, 'Who has required these things from you?', and, 'In vain do you worship Me, teaching the doctrines and traditions of men.'

ii. Even if some are not neglecting the things appointed by God to lead to mortification, they may not be using them in their proper place and order. Praying, fasting, watching, meditation, and the like, certainly have their use for the business at hand, but many consider them as the fountain and not the stream coming from the fountain. These actions are the means only, and are subordinate to the Spirit and faith. There is no merit in mere work accomplished. Many are satisfied when they fast so much, pray so much, and keep certain hours and times even if the work of mortification is not done. As the apostle says of some in another case, 'They are always learning, never coming to the knowledge of the truth.' These are always mortifying, but never come to any sound mortification. In a word, they have many means to mortify the natural man, but none to mortify lust and corruption.

This is the general mistake of men who are ignorant of the gospel. It lies at the bottom of much of the superstition and will-worship that has been brought into the world. What horrible self-afflictions have been practised by some of the ancient authors of monastic devotion! What extreme suffering they have put upon themselves. Search their objectives and you will find at the root this mistake; namely, the attempt at rigid mortification. They have fallen upon the *natural* man instead of the corrupt *old* man. They have fallen upon *the body that we live in*, instead of *the body of death*.

When men are troubled with the guilt of a sin that has prevailed over them, they promise themselves and God that they will sin thus no more, but they seek to accomplish their own victory. They watch over themselves and pray for a short season until the pain of conviction waxes cold and the sense of sin wears off. Mortification then also goes out the door, and sin returns to its former dominion.

These ways are not sufficient. There is no self-endeavour that can accomplish mortification. Almighty energy is necessary for its accomplishment.

2. *Mortification is accomplished by the Spirit.*

i. God promised His Spirit to be given to us for this very work. He takes away the stony heart – that is, the stubborn, proud, rebellious, and unbelieving heart (*Ezek.* 11:19; 36:26; *Isa.* 57:17–18).

ii. We receive mortification as a part of the blessings we receive in Christ. All the blessings that we have in Christ are given to us by the Spirit of Christ. Without Christ we can do nothing (*John* 15:5). All the blessings and graces we experience in Him at the beginning, and our growth in Him, are sent by the Spirit. He alone works in and on believers. Through His strength, sin can be mortified. Through Christ our Prince and Saviour we have repentance (*Acts* 5:31). Mortification is a significant part of repentance. How does Christ effect this in us? He does it through the promise of the Holy Spirit (*Acts* 2:33). There are manifold promises which He has made concerning the sending of the Spirit to do the works that He would see accomplished in us.

3. *How does the Spirit mortify sin?*

Let us consider three ways:

i. By causing our hearts to abound in grace and the fruits that are contrary to the works of the flesh. In

Galatians 5:19–21, Paul teaches that the fruits of the Spirit are contrary to the works of the flesh. You might ask, 'Cannot the works of the flesh and the fruits of the Spirit both abound in us?' 'No,' says he, 'they that are Christ's have crucified the flesh with the affections and lusts' (*Gal.* 5:24, AV).

'But how does the Spirit give us victory?' By our living in the Spirit and walking after the Spirit. As we abound in the graces of the Spirit and walk according to them, the fruits of the Spirit restrict the fruits of the flesh, because the works of the flesh are contrary to the works of the Spirit. This renewing of us by the Holy Spirit, as it is called (*Titus* 3:5), is one great way of mortification. He causes us to grow, thrive, flourish, and abound in the graces which are contrary, opposite, and destructive to all the works of the flesh, and contrary to the thriving of indwelling sin itself.

ii. By the effective destruction of the root and habit of sin, to weaken, destroy, and take it away. He is called a 'Spirit of judgment and of burning' (*Isa.* 4:4), in really consuming and destroying our lusts. He takes away the stony heart by an almighty work. He begins this work, as to its kind, and then carries it on by degrees. He is the fire that burns up the very root of lust.

iii. He brings the cross of Christ into the heart of a sinner by faith, and gives communion with Christ in His death, and fellowship in His sufferings.

4. *The work of the Spirit and our responsibility.*

If mortification is a work of the Holy Spirit alone, how is it that we are exhorted to accomplish it? Seeing that the Spirit of God only can do it, why not leave the work wholly to Him?

i. Other graces and good works which are in us are His working also. He 'works in [us], both to will and to work for His good pleasure' (*Phil.* 2:13). He works 'all our works in us' (*Isa.* 26:12, AV), and He works 'the work of faith with power' (*2 Thess.* 1:11, *Col.* 2:12, AV). He causes us to pray, and is a 'Spirit of supplication' (*Rom.* 8:26, *Zech.* 12:10, AV). Yet, we are exhorted to do all of these.

ii. He does not so work in us that it is not still an act of our obedience. The Holy Spirit so works in us and upon us, as we are able to be wrought in and upon, and yet He preserves our own liberty and free obedience. He works upon our understandings, wills, consciences, and affections, agreeably to their own natures. He works in us and with us, not against us or without us, so that His assistance is an encouragement as to the accomplishing of the work.

I might here bewail the endless, foolish labour of poor souls, who are convinced of sin, and yet not able to stand against its power. They try many perplexing ways and duties, to keep down sin, but, being strangers to the Spirit of God, they find it is all in vain. They combat without victory, have war without peace, and are in slavery all their days. They spend their strength for that which is not bread, and their labour for that which does not profit.

This is the saddest warfare that any poor creature can be engaged in. A soul under the power of conviction from the law is pressed to fight against sin, but he has no strength for the battle. He must fight, but he can never conquer. He is like a man who thrusts himself on the sword of the enemy on purpose to be slain. The law drives him on, and then sin beats him back. Sometimes he thinks he has foiled sin, but he has only raised a dust, so that he cannot see the sin. He stirs up his natural affections of fear, sorrow, and anguish, and this makes him believe that sin is conquered when it is not even touched. He soon must be at the battle again, and the lust which he thought to be slain is seen to be not even wounded.

If the case of these who labour and strive, and yet never enter into the kingdom of God, is sad, what is the condition of those who are not even concerned? They are those who are perpetually under the power and dominion of sin, and love to have it so. They are troubled about nothing, except to continue to make provision for the flesh and to fulfil the lusts thereof.

4

How Life and Comfort
Depend on Mortification

As we walk with our God we desire greatly His strength, comfort, power and peace. The realization of these, and thus the joy of our spiritual life, depends greatly upon the mortification of sin.

But notice:

1. *I do not say they proceed from it, as though they were necessarily tied to it.* A man may be carried on in a constant course of mortification all his days, and yet perhaps never enjoy a good day of peace and consolation. So it was with Heman in Psalm 88. His life was a life of perpetual mortification and walking with God, yet terrors and wounds were his portion all his days.

But God singled out Heman, a choice friend, to make him an example to those who afterwards should be in distress. Can we complain if it is with us as it was with Heman, that eminent servant of God? This shall be his praise to the end of the world. God makes it His prerogative to speak peace and consolation. 'I will do that work', says God, 'I will comfort him' (see *Isa.* 57:18–19). But how? By an immediate work of the new creation: 'I create it', says God. The use of means for the obtaining of peace is ours; the bestowing of it is God's prerogative.

2. *Mortification is not the immediate means that God has instituted to give us life, vigour, courage, and consolation.* The immediate cause of these privileges is our adoption. 'The Spirit himself bears witness with our spirit that we are children of God' (*Rom.* 8:16). Our spiritual life, vigour, courage and consolation, then, come at the hand of the Spirit as we sense and understand our adoption and justification. However:

3. *In our ordinary walking with God, and in the ordinary course of His dealing with us, the vigour and comfort of our spiritual lives depend much on our mortification.* Mortification not only bears a cause-and-effect relationship to our joy, but it works effectually to bring it to pass. The vigour of our spiritual lives is not possible apart from mortification.

Mortification prevents sin from depriving us of health in our spiritual life. Every unmortified sin will certainly do two things:

1. *It will weaken the soul, and deprive it of its vigour.* When David had, for a while, harboured an unmortified lust in his heart, it broke all his bones, and left him no spiritual strength; hence he complained that he was sick, weak, wounded, faint. 'There is', he said, 'no soundness in my flesh' (*Psa.* 38:3); 'I am feeble and crushed' (verse 8). Indeed, I cannot so much as 'look up' (*Psa.* 40:12, AV). An unmortified lust will drink up the spirit, and all the vigour of the soul, and weaken it for all duties. For:

i. Sin untunes and unframes the heart itself, by entangling its affections. It diverts the heart from the spiritual frame that is required for vigorous communion with God. It lays hold on the affections, rendering its object beloved and desirable, so expelling the love of the Father (*1 John* 2:15; 3:17). The unmortified soul cannot say uprightly and truly that God is its portion, having something else that it loves. The soul and its affections, that should be full of God, cannot be full of Him, since it is entangled in worldly pursuits.

ii. Sin fills the thoughts with its enticements. First it captures the thoughts and, if unmortified, it then seeks to make provision for and fulfil the lusts of the flesh.

iii. Sin breaks out and actually hinders duty. The ambitious man must be studying, the worldling must be working or contriving, and the sensual, vain person providing vanity for himself, when they should be engaged in the worship of God. It would extend this discourse too much to set forth the breaches, ruin, weakness, and desolations that one unmortified lust will bring upon a soul.

2. *Sin will also darken the soul, and deprive it of its comfort and peace.* Sin darkens the soul. It is a cloud, a thick cloud, that spreads itself over the face of the soul, and intercepts all the beams of God's love and favour. It takes away all sense of the privilege of our adoption; and if the soul begins to gather up thoughts of consolation, sin quickly scatters them.

Mortification prunes all the graces of God, and makes room for them in our hearts to grow. The life and vigour of our spiritual life consists in the vigour and flourishing of the plants of grace in our hearts. Now, as you may see in a garden, let there be a precious herb planted, and let the ground be untilled, and weeds grow about it, perhaps it will live still, but it will be a poor, withering and unuseful thing. You must look and search for it, and sometimes can scarce find it; and when you do, you can scarce know it, whether it is the plant you look for or not; and suppose it is, you can make no use of it at all. But let another of the same kind be set in the ground, naturally as barren and bad as the other, but let it be well weeded, and every thing that is noxious and hurtful removed from it, it flourishes and thrives; you may see it at first glance into the garden, and have it for your use when you please.

So it is with the graces of the Spirit that are planted in our hearts. If they abide in a heart where there is some neglect of mortification, and they are about to die (*Rev.* 3: 2), they are withering and decaying. The heart is like the sluggard's field, so overgrown with weeds that you can scarce see the good corn. Such a man may search for faith, love, and zeal, and scarce be able to find any. If he does discover that these graces are there and alive, yet they are so weak and so clogged with lusts, they are of very little use; they remain, indeed, but are ready to die.

But now let the heart be cleansed by mortification, and the weeds of lust constantly and daily rooted up (as they spring daily, nature being their proper soil), there will be room for grace to thrive and flourish, the graces that God gives will act their part, and be ready for every use and purpose!

5

What Mortification
Is Not

Suppose a man is a true believer, and yet finds in himself a powerful indwelling sin. This sin makes him captive to its power, and consumes his heart with trouble. It perplexes his thoughts, weakens his soul in communion with God, takes away his peace, defiles his conscience, and exposes him to hardening through the deceitfulness of sin. What shall he do? What course shall he take to mortify this sin, lust, or corruption? How can he gain victory enough, even though it is not utterly destroyed, yet, in his contest with it, he may be enabled to maintain his power, strength, and peace in communion with God?

We must first consider what mortification is not.

1. *To mortify a sin is not to utterly root it out and destroy it*, that it should have no more hold at all nor

residence in our hearts. It is true that this is what we aim at, but we will not be able to accomplish it in this life. All who seek mortification seek the utter destruction, both of its fruit and its root in the heart and life. They seek to kill it, so that it will never move nor stir any more, nor cry, call, seduce or tempt, to all eternity. We aim at the total destruction of the sin, so that it does not exist.

There may doubtless be times of wonderful success by the Spirit and grace of Christ, and such a great victory that a man may have almost constant triumph over it; but the utter killing and destruction of it, we cannot expect in this life. Paul, who was a choice saint and a pattern for believers in faith, love, and all the fruits of the Spirit, who had no equal in the world, himself said: 'Not that I have already obtained this or am already perfect' (*Phil.* 3:12).

He still had a lowly body as we have, which must be changed by the great power of Christ at last. We are complete only in Christ, not in ourselves (*Col.* 2:10).

2. *Mortification is not just the changing of some outward aspects of a sin.* There may be an apparent change of life. God however knows the heart. Someone may change an obvious sin for a hidden one. Mortification is not just the substitution of one sin for another. He may simply have changed from one road to hell to a safer path than he was on before. He may have a different heart than he had, one which is more cunning; not a new heart, which is more holy!

3. *Mortification is not just the improvement of our natural constitution.* Some men have an advantage in their natural temperament over others. They do not have the violence of unruly passions and affections that many others have. Let these men cultivate and improve their natural frame and temper by discipline, and they may seem to themselves and others very mortified men. It may be, however, that their hearts are a standing sink of all abominations.

Someone may not have so much trouble all his life, perhaps with anger and passion, as others, and yet not advance as far in true mortification. Our natural tempers are not a good test for true mortification. Let those with gentle natural temperaments consider the need for self-denial, or such spiritual sins as unbelief and envy, to get a better view of their true selves.

4. *A sin is not mortified when it is only diverted.* Simon Magus left his sorceries for a while, but then he turned to covetousness and ambition. Peter thus told him, 'I see that you are in the gall of bitterness.' Even though he had made a profession and had given up his sorceries, his lust was as powerful as ever; it was the same lust, only the streams of it were diverted in a different direction. It was exerting itself in another way, but it was the old gall of bitterness still. A man may be aware of a lust and set himself against the outbreakings of it, but in the meantime suffer the same corrupted habit to vent itself in some other way.

It is like one who heals a sore in the body, only to have it break out in another location. This diversion, with the various alterations that go with it, is common among those who have not experienced grace. In the natural progress of life there are changes in men's interests and goals, and these may set a man in a different direction. As men grow older they do not usually persist in the pursuit of youthful lusts, although they have never mortified any one of them. One may leave one lust, so that he may serve another. He that changes pride for worldliness, or sensuality for legalism, does damage to himself and others. Let him not think that he has mortified the sin that he seems to have left. He has changed his master, but is a servant still.

5. *Occasional victories over sin are not mortification.* There are two occasions or seasons in which a man who is fighting with a particular sin may seem to have mortified it, but has not in reality.

i. When that sin breaks out sadly and seriously in a way that greatly disturbs his peace, terrifies his conscience, brings the dread of scandal, and clearly provokes the Lord to judgment. This may awaken and stir up all that is in that man, filling him with the abhorrence of sin, and sending him to God to cry out for life and help to set himself against the sin. The whole man, both spiritual and natural, is aroused. Sin shrinks. The sin in question appears to lie dead before him. It is like a soldier who draws near the enemy lines and kills an important person.

The guards then awake and make strict inquiry after the enemy. The enemy, meanwhile, has hidden himself like one that is dead until the noise and tumult is over. Though for the time being he is quiet, there is in his mind the firm resolution to do more mischief at the first opportunity.

See how the Corinthians muster up a sudden attempt to destroy the sin that is among them (2 Cor. 7:11). So it is when a lust has broken out in actual sin, destroying a man's peace of conscience. Carefulness, indignation, desire, fear, revenge, are all set to work against it. Lust is quiet for a season, being put down by these temporary weapons. When the hurry is over, and the inquest is past, the thief appears again alive, and is as busy as ever at his work.

ii. In a time of some great trial, calamity, or pressing affliction, when the heart is taken up with escaping the present troubles, fears, and dangers, a person may resolve to relinquish his sin and so gain peace with God. To gain freedom from the affliction, he concludes that he must obtain victory over sin. Some in this situation may resolve that sin shall never have any place in them and that they will never give themselves over to it from now on. Sin thus is quiet, does not stir, and seems to be mortified. However, it has not received a mortal wound, and has merely been temporarily suppressed. When the fear of trial and affliction ceases to occupy the thoughts, the sin returns again to its former life and vigour.

'In spite of all this, they still sinned;
Despite his wonders they did not believe.
So he made their days vanish like a breath,
And their years in terror.
When he killed them, they sought him;
They repented and sought God earnestly.
They remembered that God was their rock,
The Most High God their redeemer.
But they flattered him with their mouths;
They lied to him with their tongue.
Their heart was not steadfast towards him,
They were not faithful to his covenant' (*Psa.* 78:32–37).

I do not doubt that when they sought Him, and returned, and inquired earnestly after God, that they did so fully purposing in their hearts to relinquish their sins. This is clear in the word 'repented', or, as it is in the Hebrew, 'returned'. To turn or return to the Lord implies the relinquishment of sin. They did this earnestly and diligently. Their sin however was still unmortified, even after all this. Days spent in affliction and humiliation can be a great deception to believers.

These are some of the ways, and there are many others, whereby poor souls deceive themselves, and suppose they have mortified their lusts when they are still alive, mighty, and seeking at every opportunity to break forth to disrupt and disturb the soul's peace.

6

What Mortification Is

The mortification of a lust consists in three things:

1. *A habitual weakening of the lust.*

Every lust is a depraved habit or inclination pushing the heart toward evil. Genesis 6:5 describes the man who has not mortified his lust: 'Every imagination of the thoughts of his heart is only evil continually.' This man is always under the power of a strong bent and inclination toward sin. The reason that the natural man does not always pursue a single lust night and day is because he has so many different lusts to serve. Each one is crying out to be satisfied.

Even though a lust is not always exerting an influence on our imagination and thoughts, we should consider that lust that we seek to mortify a strong and deeply rooted habitual inclination and bent of the will and affections. Men are said to have their 'hearts set upon evil', and the inclination in their spirit is to make 'provision for the flesh' (*Rom.* 13:14).

Our moral and holy habits exert themselves differently from lust. Moral habits speak to the soul gently and appropriately as they should. Sinful and depraved habits arrive with violence and impetuousness. These lusts are said to fight or wage 'war against [the] soul' (*1 Pet.* 2:11). They rebel and rise up, demanding their fulfilment. See also Romans 7:23, in which sin is said to take a man captive to accomplish its goal.

From the description we have in Romans 7, lust darkens the mind, extinguishes convictions, dethrones reason, interrupts the power and influences that resist it, and then breaks out into an open flame.

Important distinctions about the nature of lust:

One lust in a man may prove to be much stronger than another lust might be in the same man. A particular lust might also be stronger in one man than in another man. Certain lusts may be strengthened by the natural constitutions and temperaments of particular persons. Also, opportunity enflames the strength of a lust. Satan has thousands of ways to support a lust so that it grows violent and impetuous above other lusts. The strength of the lust darkens the mind so that the knowledge that once might have resisted exerts no power over the will, so that the lust finds freedom to express itself.

In particular, lust gets its strength by temptation. When a suitable temptation falls in line with a lust, the lust obtains a new life, vigour, power, violence and rage that it did not seem capable of before.

Some lusts are more obvious than others, and more serious in their outcome. Paul distinguishes sexual immorality from other sins:

'Flee from sexual immorality. Every other sin a person commits is outside the body, but the sexually immoral person sins against his own body' (1 Cor. 6:18).

Other sins perhaps, such as the love of the world, may be just as strong and predominant in a man, but they do not do as much damage to the whole man.

With this in mind, a particular man may appear, in comparison with others, to be a mortified man. In reality however, his lust is just as strong, though not as apparent. His lust may not be as outwardly scandalous as others, but it is lust just the same. It may not disturb the soul as violently as other sins, but it nevertheless controls him as he secretly harbours it.

The weakening of lust: The first thing in mortification is the weakening of the habit of sin or lust, so that it shall not, with that violence, earnestness and frequency, rise up and conceive, provoke, entice, and disquiet as it naturally has a tendency to do (*James* 1:14–15). This is called 'crucifying the flesh with its passions and desires' (*Gal.* 5:24). We seek to take away that about it which gives it its strength and power. We aim at the killing of the body of death 'day by day' (see 2 Cor. 4:16).

When a man is nailed to a cross, he at first struggles, strives, and cries out with great strength and might; but as his blood and spirits waste, his strivings are faint and seldom, his cries low and hoarse, and scarce to be heard. So when a man first determines to conquer a lust or sin, and to deal with it in earnest, it struggles with great violence to break loose; it cries with earnestness and impatience to be satisfied and relieved. By mortification, the blood and spirits of it are let out, it moves seldom and faintly, cries sparingly, and is scarce heard in the heart; it may sometimes have a dying pang that makes an appearance of great vigour and strength, but it is quickly over, especially if it is kept from considerable success.

This Paul describes in Romans 6. Sin, he says, is crucified; it is fastened to the cross. To what end? 'That the body of sin might be brought to nothing.' The power of sin is weakened and abolished little by little, so that we should 'no longer be enslaved to sin'; that is, so that sin should not be our master and control us as before. This includes not only our fleshly desires, but those of the mind and the will which are in opposition to God.

With all troubling sin, no matter whether it encourages us to do evil or hinders us from doing good, the rule is the same: it must be mortified or it will arise again. A man may beat down the bitter fruit from an evil tree until he is weary but while the root of the tree continues to abide in strength and vigour, the beating down of the present fruit will not hinder it from bearing more evil fruit. This is the folly of some men; they set themselves with all earnestness and diligence against the breaking out of a lust, but they leave the principle and root untouched. They will make little or no progress in this work of true mortification.

2. *A constant fight and contention against sin.*

To be able to fight effectively against sin is a large part of its mortification. When sin is strong and vigorous, the soul finds it difficult to make headway against it. The inner man sighs, groans, mourns and is troubled at its force. David complains that his sin had overtaken him so that he could not see (*Psa.* 40:12). How little, then, was he able to fight against it!

Three things are required in this fighting against sin:

(i.) We need to recognize the enemy we are dealing with and resolve that it is to be destroyed by all means possible. The battle is a vigorous and hazardous one that deals with the issues of eternity. When a man is not very concerned, and sees his lust as a trivial thing, it is an indication that he is not mortified or even heading in that direction.

We cannot go forward unless we recognize the plague of our own hearts (*1 Kings* 8:38, AV). It is to be feared that too many do not realize the enemy that they carry about with them in their hearts. This makes them ready to justify themselves, and to be impatient when they are reproved or admonished. They do not begin to realize the danger they are in (see *2 Chron.* 16:10).

ii. We need to be intimately acquainted with the ways, wiles, methods, advantages, and occasions which give lust its success. This is how men deal with their enemies. They search out their plans, ponder their goals, and consider how and by what means they have prevailed over them in the past. Then they can be defeated. Without this kind of strategic thinking, warfare is very primitive. Those who indeed mortify lust deal with it in this way. Even when lust is not enticing and seducing, they consider, while at leisure, 'This is still our enemy; this is his way and his methods, these are his advantages, this is the way he has prevailed, and he will do this, if he is not prevented.'

One of the choicest and most important parts of spiritual wisdom is to find out the subtleties, policies, and depths of any indwelling sin; to consider where its greatest strength lies – how it uses occasions, opportunities, and temptations to gain an advantage. We need to find out its pleas, pretences and reasonings, and see what its strategies, disguises and excuses are! We need to set the Spirit against the craft of the old man; to trace this serpent in all of its turning and windings, and to bring its most secret tricks out into the open. We must learn to say; 'This is your usual method; I know what you are up to.' So to be always ready is the beginning of our warfare.

iii. We need to continue to attack our lusts daily with the spiritual weapons that are most detrimental to it. This is the key to the warfare. Even when we think that a lust is dead because it is quiet, we must labour to give it new wounds and new blows every day (*Col.* 3:5).

[37]

When the soul is in this condition and dealing in this way with lust, it has the upper hand. Sin is under the sword and is dying.

3. *A degree of success in the battle.*

Frequent success against any lust strengthens us and gives the evidence of mortification. By success I do not mean a mere disappointment of sin, in that it is not put into practice. By success I mean gaining full victory over it and pursuing it for a complete conquest. For instance, when the heart at any time recognizes sin and temptation in action, seducing it and forming sinful imaginations to put the lust into practice, the heart must immediately see what is happening, bring the sin to the law of God and the love of Christ, condemn it, and follow it to execute it to the uttermost.

When a man comes to this state and condition, his lust is weakened at the root and principle. Sin's activity and actions are now fewer and weaker than formerly, and sin is not able to hinder man's duty nor interrupt his peace. When man can quietly and in a calm frame of spirit search out and fight against sin and gain the victory against it, and continue in the peace of God; then sin is mortified in some considerable measure.

Thus, our victory of mortification will be realized to a large extent as we weaken lust's presence and entice-ments. We must implant, promote the continual residence of, and cherish those graces that stand in direct oppos-ition to the lust. So, for example, by the implanting and growth of humility, pride is weakened. Passion is weakened by patience, uncleanness by purity of mind and conscience, and love of this world by heavenly-mindedness. These graces of the Spirit, as they are expressed in various ways, weaken the perplexing lusts that wage their warfare against us.

Our victory will be further realized as the new man immediately springs to action, and cheerfully fights against lust the moment it appears. We must use every weapon available to conquer it!

These weapons will secure a great degree of success. If a particular sin does not have some unusual advantage as a result of its nature, then the victory gained may become a permanent conquest. The soul may thus arrive at a great degree of peace of conscience, according to the terms of the covenant of grace.

7

Only Believers Can
Mortify Sin

What are the ways and means in which a soul might proceed to mortify any particular lust or sin? Let us consider general rules and principles that are necessary to gain true victory in our battle for mortification.

The first rule is this:

Unless a man is a true believer, and grafted into Christ, he can never mortify a single sin. Mortification is the work of believers: 'If by the Spirit you . . .' (*Rom.* 8:13), that is, you *believers*, to whom there is no condemnation, (verse 1). Only believers are exhorted to mortification: 'Put to death therefore what is earthly in you' (*Col.* 3:5). Who should mortify? You who 'have been raised with Christ' (verse 1), and whose 'life is hidden with Christ in God', who also will 'appear with him in glory' (verse 4).

An unregenerate man may do something like mortification, but the real work itself, so that it may be acceptable with God, he can never perform. Some of the philosophers declare how they have conquered the world and self, and are able to regulate their affections and passions! The lives however of most of them reveal that their boasts differ from true mortification just as the sun which is painted upon a fence differs from the sun itself; it has neither light nor heat. There is no death of sin without the death of Christ. You realize how the Papists, in their vows and penances seek mortification according to the principles of their church, yet they are like Israel who, seeking for their own righteousness, have not attained it! Why? Because they seek it by works of the law and not by faith (*Rom.* 9:31–32).

It is the duty of every person, whoever hears the gospel or law preached, to mortify sin. It is his duty! But it is not his *immediate* duty; he must do it in God's way. A servant who is directed to pay a bill must first collect the money at the bank. It is his duty to pay the bill, but he must first collect the money before he obeys this injunction. So it is in this case; sin is to be mortified, but something is to be done in the first place to enable us carry it out.

We have seen that the Spirit alone can truly mortify sin; He has promised to do it, and all other means without Him are empty and vain. How shall we mortify sin if we do not even have the Holy Spirit? How do we receive the Holy Spirit? Paul said that if we do not have the Spirit of Christ, we do not belong to Him (*Rom.* 8:9). If we are

Christ's, and have an interest in Him, we indeed have the Spirit, and have the power for mortification. We see however that those without Christ cannot please God: 'Those who are in the flesh cannot please God' (*Rom.* 8:8). The natural man is in a state of enmity with God and his law. In this state it is impossible to please Him! Man is only delivered from this condition by the Spirit of Christ. 'You, however, are not in the flesh but in the Spirit, if in fact the Spirit of God dwells in you' (*Rom.* 8:9). Our union with Christ and the power of the Spirit enable us to mortify sin. All attempts at mortification without a true interest in Christ are vain!

Many men are troubled with the guilt of sin. At times the arrows of conviction are piercing to the natural man. He may be brought to a state of concern from preaching or some great affliction. He may set himself against a particular lust that greatly disturbs his peace of heart. But the poor creature! He labours in the fire, and his efforts are destroyed. When the Spirit of Christ comes to the work, He works 'like a refiner's fire' and he will purge men as gold and silver (*Mal.* 3:2–3), take away their dross and tin, their filth and blood (see also *Isa.* 4:4). BUT men must be gold and silver before the refiner's fire will work. The prophet gives us the outcome of a wicked man's effort for self-mortification: 'The bellows blow fiercely; the lead is consumed by the fire; in vain the refining goes on, for the wicked are not removed. Rejected silver they are called, for the LORD has rejected them' (*Jer.* 6:29–30) What is the reason? Verse 28: they were bronze and iron when they were put into the furnace. Men may refine bronze and iron forever, but they will not become good silver.

Mortification is not the present duty of unregenerate men. God calls them to conversion first. He calls them to the conversion of their whole soul, not just the mortification of this or that particular lust. You might laugh at a man that would build without a foundation. Each day that he builds his previous day's work falls down. Look at him as he continues in the same course day by day. So it is with those who seek mortification without salvation. What progress they make one day they lose another day, and yet they continue in this course and do not ask themselves where the flaw in their progress might be found.

On the day of Pentecost the Jews who cried out 'What shall we do?' were directed by Peter toward conversion and faith in Christ. He did not bid them to go and mortify their pride, wrath, malice, cruelty, and the like. So let the soul first be thoroughly converted and then humiliation and mortification will ensue. John also came preaching repentance and conversion. The Pharisees had been laying heavy burdens, imposing tedious duties, and rigid means of mortification, in fastings, washings, and the like, but all in vain. The Saviour also tells us what is to be done in such a case: If the tree is made good, its fruit will be good (*Matt.* 12:33). The root must be dealt with, the nature of the tree changed, or no good fruit will be brought forth!

Thus, unless a man is regenerated and a true believer, all his attempts at mortification are to no purpose. His attempts may be great and promising, he may use all the means available, he may seek it with much diligence, earnestness, watchfulness, and strict attention of mind and spirit, but in vain he labours. He shall not be healed. Seeking mortification without regeneration presents serious problems to those so engaged. Let us consider three:

1. *The mind and soul are diverted from that which is most important.* The business at hand for the sinner must be to consider his serious condition. He needs to apply himself toward conversion. God stirs our conscience and disquiets our heart that we might recognize our need of Him. Seeking mortification of sin just to quiet the soul and find relief from the torment of the conscience, all the while neglecting to deal with the root cause of sin, is a result of self-love. Men are diverted from coming to God in this way. This is one of the most common deceptions in which men ruin their souls. They seek to apply themselves to victory over the troubling sin but do not allow their conviction to lead them to the gospel. They perish in their 'reformation'.

2. *This duty, being a good thing in itself and in its proper place, tends to bring a false peace to the conscience.* A person is ready to conclude that his state and condition are good. This is a delusion. When a man's conscience is made sick with sin, and can find no rest, he needs to go to the great Physician of souls and get healing in His blood. But if that man is able to quiet his conscience through 'victory' over a sin, he sits down without

going to Christ at all. How many souls are thus deceived, right on into eternity! How many religions are designed to pacify the conscience without Christ (*Rom.* 10:3)! By this means men satisfy themselves that their state and condition is good. They are hardened in a kind of self-righteousness.

3. *When a man has for a season such soul deception, and then finds out after the long course of his life that his sin was not truly mortified, or that he has just changed one sin for another, he begins to believe that victory over sin is impossible.* Fighting against it he now sees as vain. He may then yield himself over to the power of the sin, believing that success is impossible.

Such an attempt to mortify sin without Christ deludes, hardens, and destroys the sinner. There are usually no more vile sinners than those who have chosen this course, found it fruitless, and deserted it without the discovery of Christ. Mortification is the work of believers, and believers only! To kill sin is the work of living men; where men are dead (as all unbelievers, even the best of them, are), sin is alive, and will live.

This, then, is a general rule: Be sure to get an interest in Christ; for if you attempt to mortify any sin without it, it will never be done. If a task can be accomplished only with one instrument, it would be madness for one to seek to accomplish it without using that instrument.

OBJECTION: One might say, 'What, then, would you have unregenerate men that are convinced of the evil of sin do?

Shall they cease striving against sin, and live without restraint, give way to their lusts, and be as bad as the worst of men? Would not this be the way to set the whole world into confusion, bringing it into darkness, open the flood gates of lust, and push men into all sin with delight and greediness, like a horse plunging into battle?'

Answer 1. God forbid! God in His wisdom, goodness, and love uses various means that keep the sons of men from running into such excess of riot and lust. Without this the whole earth would be a hell of sin and confusion.

Answer 2. There is a powerful working of the Word of God in the world that humbles sinners and restrains them in their sin, though they are never converted. This happens even though the purpose of the Word preached is conversion and not just restraint.

Answer 3. Even though this restraining of sin is the outcome of the preaching of the Word and the work of the Holy Spirit, and it is a good work, those who are not converted are still under the power of darkness.

Answer 4. We must let men know that mortification is their duty, but in its proper place; I do not encourage men to come away from mortification, but to come to conversion. He that shall call a man from mending a hole in the wall of his house, to quench a fire that is consuming the whole building, is not his enemy. Poor soul! It is not your sore finger but your great fever you need to notice. You set yourself against a particular sin, and do not realize that you are nothing but sin.

Advice to Preachers:
It is the duty of preachers to plead with men about their sins, but we must always remember to speak in such a way as to lead them to the discovery of their state and condition. Otherwise we may lead men to formality and hypocrisy and not accomplish the true end of preaching the gospel. It will not avail to beat a man off from his drunkenness into a sober formality. We must lay the axe at the root. To deal with sin without the root is like beating an enemy in the open field, and chasing him into an impregnable castle where he cannot be touched. Drive the conviction to the heart, not just particular sins.

We must not call men to mortification, but to believing. Vows and the like to mortify sin, apart from saving grace, commonly make lust more impetuous. If victory is not gained, even for a season, it increases their guilt and torment. Is not mortification without conversion like making bricks without straw? How can an unregenerate man find assistance for the performance of this task?

Can sin be truly killed without an interest in the death of Christ, and the work of the Spirit? If such directions should prevail to change men's lives, as seldom they do, they never will reach to the change of their hearts! They just make men self-justified or hypocrites, and not Christians.

It grieves me often to see poor souls that have a zeal for God and a desire of eternal welfare, kept by such teachers under a hard, burdensome, and outward worship and service of God. They have many endeavours for mortification, but an ignorance of the righteousness of Christ and the work of the Spirit. If God ever shines in their hearts to give them the knowledge of His glory in the face of His Son Jesus Christ, they will see the folly of their present way.

8

God Requires Universal Obedience

The second general rule is this: *You cannot mortify a specific lust that is troubling you, unless you are seeking to obey the Lord from the heart in all areas!*

Suppose a man finds a particular lust to be powerful, strong, and violent. It takes him captive. He is troubled by it and it takes away his peace. He is not able to bear it; and sets himself against it, prays against it, groans under it, and sighs to be delivered. BUT in the meantime, perhaps, in other duties, in constant communion with God, in reading, prayer, and meditation, and in other ways, he is loose and negligent. He will not then be able to gain the victory over that troubling lust. This is a common condition among the sons of men in their pilgrimage.

Israel drew near to God with much diligence and earnestness. They fasted and prayed. 'They seek me daily and delight to know my ways . . . they ask of me right-eous judgments; they delight to draw near to God' (*Isa.* 58:2). But God rejected it all. Their fast was not enough to heal them. Verses 5–7 tell why. This was the only duty they observed! They attended diligently to this one, but in the others they were negligent and careless.

If a man has a discharging sore as a result of a bad physical state, and if he seeks to heal the sore without correcting the underlying state, he will labour in vain. So it is with our spiritual nature. If we seek to correct an out-break of sin in the soul, but neglect the basic duties that promote our spirituality, we labour in vain. For:

1. *This endeavour for mortification has a bad foun-dation.* We must hate all sin, as sin, and not just that which troubles us. Love for Christ, because He went to the cross, and hate for sin that sent Him there, is the solid foundation for true spiritual mortification. To seek mor-tification only because a sin troubles us proceeds from self-love. Why do you with all diligence and earnestness seek to mortify this sin? Because it troubles you and takes away your peace, and fills your heart with sorrow, trouble, and fear, and because you do not have rest through it? Yes, but, friend, you have neglected prayer and reading! You have been vain and loose in your con-versation with other things. These are just as sinful as the one that troubles you. Jesus Christ bled for them also. Why do you not set yourself against them? If you hate sin as sin, and every evil way, you would be watchful against

everything that grieves and disquiets the Spirit of God. You would not be concerned only about the sin that upsets your own soul! It is evident that you fight against this sin merely because it troubles you. If it did not bother your conscience you would let it alone. If it did not bother you, you would not bother it. Do you think God will help you in such a hypocritical effort? Do you think that the Holy Spirit will help in the treachery and falsehood of your own spirit? Do you think he will free you from this so you are free to go and commit another sin which grieves Him?

'No', says God, 'If I free him from this lust, I will not hear from him any more, and he will be content in his failure.' We must not be concerned only with that which troubles us, but with all that troubles God. God's work is to have full victory, and universal obedience, not just the victory over the sins which trouble our soul.

'Let us cleanse ourselves from every defilement of body and spirit, bringing holiness to completion in the fear of God' (*2 Cor.* 7:1).

If we will do anything, we must do everything. So, then, our need is not only an intense opposition to this or that particular lust, but a universal humble frame and temper of heart that watches over every evil, and seeks the performance of every duty that is pleasing to God.

2. *Maybe God has allowed this troubling lust to have power over you to draw your attention to other failures and your lukewarmness in walking before Him.* He at

least has allowed it to trouble you to awaken you to consider your ways. Maybe this troubling will lead to a thorough work and change in your course, to walk fully with God.

The troubling of a particular lust is a common fruit and outcome of a careless and negligent course in general. Consider two reasons:

1. *This is a natural effect.* Lust lies in the heart of every one, even the best while he lives. Scripture also teaches that lust is subtle, cunning, crafty, that it seduces, entices, fights, and rebels. While a man keeps a diligent watch over his heart, lust withers and dies in it. But, through negligence, lust erupts in some particular way. Lust takes opportunity through the thoughts or desires and breaks out into open sin. When lust finds its expression in a particular avenue it keeps pushing, vexing, and disquieting the soul. In such a case it is not so easily restrained. A man may find himself wrestling with it in sorrow all his days. By a diligent spiritual watch, this might have been easily prevented.

2. *God often suffers a particular lust to chasten our other negligences.* As with wicked men, He gives them up to one sin as the judgment of another, a greater for the punishment of a less, or one that will hold them more firmly and securely for that from which they might possibly have obtained a deliverance (*Rom.* 1:26). Even so with His children, He might leave them in one trouble to

cure another evil. Such was the messenger of Satan let loose on Paul that he might not be lifted up through the abundance of his spiritual revelations (*2 Cor.* 12:7). Was it not a correction to Peter's vain confidence that he was left to deny his Master? Now, if this is the case, that God suffers one sin to prevail to admonish us, to humble us, and perhaps to chasten and correct us, then how can we expect to put down that troubling sin without dealing with the root cause? We need to realize that our general course must be reformed.

He who truly and thoroughly seeks to mortify any disquieting lust, must be equally diligent in all parts of obedience. We must see that every lust and every omission of duty is a burden to God. If we do not seek to obey in every area of our lives, our soul becomes weak. If we seek only to have victory over the sin that troubles us, and do not consider the filth and guilt of it, we are selfish and offer a constant provocation to God. There will not be any positive outcome to the spiritual duties we undertake, and we will not gain the victory over this great lust, if we do not seek *universal obedience*.

9

The Dangerous Symptoms of Sin

I intend now to consider specific directions for the soul seeking to gain victory over disquieting lusts. First we shall consider nine preparatory directions, and then two directions that deal directly with mortification.

PREPARATORY DIRECTION 1: *Consider the symptoms that accompany a lust*. If they are deadly and serious, then extraordinary remedies must be used. The ordinary course of mortification will not work.

Let us consider six deadly and serious symptoms:

1. *Firm establishment over a long period of time and settlement as a habitual practice*. If a sin has been corrupting your heart for a long time, and you have allowed it to

prevail and abide in power, without vigorously attempting to kill it, and heal the wounds that it causes, this is a serious condition. Have you permitted worldliness and ambition to divert you from the important duties that promote communion with God for a long season? Have you allowed unclean thoughts to defile your heart with vain, foolish, and wicked imaginations for many days? This is a serious and dangerous symptom. 'My wounds stink and fester because of my foolishness' (*Psa.* 38:5).

When a lust has remained a long time in the heart, corrupting, festering, and poisoning, it brings the soul into a woeful condition. In this instance an ordinary course of humiliation will not be sufficient. Such a lust will make a deep imprint on the soul. It will make its company a habit in your affections. It will grow so familiar to your mind and conscience that they are not disturbed at its presence as some strange thing. It will so take advantage in such a state that it will often exert itself without you even taking notice of it at all. Unless a serious and extraordinary course is taken, a person in this state has no grounds to expect that his latter end shall be peace.

How will such a person be able to distinguish between the long abode of an unmortified lust and the dominion of sin, which cannot happen to a regenerate person? And how can he hope that it will ever be any different with him when he sees his lust fixed and abiding for so long? It may be that great afflictions or mercies did not dislodge it, even though these gained the special attention of your soul. These lusts may have weathered many a storm and prevailed under the display of a variety of ministries of the Word of God. If this is the case, do you think it will prove an easy thing to dislodge such a room-mate, pleading to stay? Old and neglected wounds can prove to be fatal, and are always dangerous. Indwelling lusts grow rusty and stubborn because they have long continued in ease and quiet. Such a sin will not be easily ejected. It will never die by itself, and if it is not daily killed it will only gather added strength.

2. Another dangerous symptom is when the heart pleads to be thought in a good state, yet all the while allows the continuance of a lust without any attempt at its mortification.

Consider two ways in which this may be done:

i. When a perplexing thought of sin comes, a man, instead of applying himself to the destruction of it, searches his heart to find some good thing so that it may go well with him, even though the sin or lust continues to abide in his heart.

For a man to gather up his good experiences with God, to call them to mind, to collect them, consider them, and to try and improve them is an excellent thing. It is a duty that is rightly to be practised by all saints. It is commended in the Old and New Testaments. This was David's work when he communed with his own heart (*Psa.* 77:6–9), and called to remembrance the former loving-kindnesses of the Lord. This is the duty that Paul exhorts us to practise in 2 Corinthians 13:5. Since this is

in itself an excellent practice, so it is even more h
during a time of trial or in effort to combat sin. It is like a
picture of silver setting off the golden apple, as Solomon
describes it.

To do it, however, to satisfy your conscience when your
heart is convicted of sin is a desperate device of the heart
that is in love with sin. When a man's conscience shall
deal with him, and when God shall rebuke him for the
sinful distemper of his heart, if he, instead of applying
himself to get that sin pardoned in the blood of Christ
and mortified by His Spirit, seeks to calm his heart and
justify himself by thinking on the good he has, or thinks
he has, and so disentangles himself from the yoke of conviction that God has placed upon his neck, his condition
is very dangerous and his wound hardly curable. Thus the
Jews, under the conviction of their consciences by the
preaching of our Saviour supported themselves in the plea
that they were 'Abraham's children', and so accepted of
God. Thus they continued in abominable wickedness, to
their utter ruin.

A person who seeks peace on any account and is content to live away from the love of God in this life, so long
as it does not mean a final separation, shows that his love
for sin exceeds his love for God. What is to be expected
from such a heart?

ii. This deceit is also carried on by one who applies
grace and mercy to a sin they are not seeking to mortify.
This is a sign of a heart greatly entangled with the love of
sin. When a man has thoughts in his heart like Naaman,

saying in effect, 'In all other things I will walk with God, but in this thing, God be merciful to me' (see *2 Kings* 5:18), his condition is sad. To indulge in sin on account of mercy is altogether inconsistent with Christian sincerity. It is the badge of a hypocrite and is 'perverting the grace of our God into sensuality' (*Jude* 4). I do not doubt that, through the craft of Satan and their own remaining un-belief, the children of God may themselves sometimes be ensnared with this deceit of sin, or else Paul would never have so cautioned them against it as he does (*Rom.* 6:1–2). It is natural for the flesh to reason for itself in the light of grace and mercy. It stands ready to pervert grace for its own corrupt aims and purposes. To apply mercy to a sin not vigorously mortified is to fulfil the end of the flesh against the gospel of grace.

In these and many other ways a deceitful heart will seek to justify itself in its abominations. When a man is in such a state, and the secret liking of a sin prevails in his heart, though he doesn't give himself wholly to it, he would do so, if certain considerations did not hinder him. When such a man relieves his conscience by ways other than by true mortification and pardon in the blood of Christ, his 'wounds stink and fester', and he will, without speedy deliverance, soon be at the door of death.

3. *A third dangerous symptom is when sin frequently succeeds in obtaining the consent of the will.* When the will finds delight in a sin, even though it is not outwardly performed, the temptation is successful. A man may not

go along with the sin as to the outward act, yet if he embraces the desire of it in his heart, the temptation has prevailed. If a lust frequently succeeds in this way, it is a very bad sign. The man may be unregenerate. At any rate he is in a very dangerous condition.

The responsibility of such sin is the same regardless of whether the failure is due to the choice of the will or to spiritual negligence. Spiritual negligence itself is really a choice. The fact that our sin results from negligence does not make it less serious. We may not resolve to be negligent, but if we choose ways that lead in that direction, we are responsible for our choice. Men should not think that evil in their hearts is less serious because they are surprised that it arises. It is their neglect of watching over their hearts that causes them to be surprised.

4. *A fourth dangerous symptom is when a man fights against a sin only because of the consequences or penalty of that sin.* This is an evidence that sin has a great grip on his will, and his heart is full of wickedness. A man who only opposes the sin in his heart for fear of shame among men or eternal punishment from God would practise the sin if there were no punishment attending it. How does this differ from living in the practice of the sin? Those who belong to Christ, and are obedient to the Word of God, have the death of Christ, the love of God, the detestable nature of sin, the preciousness of communion with God, and a deep-rooted hatred of sin *as sin* to oppose to all the workings of lust in their hearts.

Consider Joseph: 'How can I do this great wickedness and sin against God?', my good and gracious God (*Gen.* 39:9). Also Paul: 'The love of Christ controls us'; and, 'Since we have these promises . . . let us cleanse ourselves from every defilement of body and spirit' (*2 Cor.* 7:1).

If a man is under the power of his lust to the extent that the only opposition to it is the law, and the arms of the law, hell and judgment, and cannot fight against it with gospel weapons, it is very evident that sin has control over his will and affections, and has prevailed and conquered.

Such a person has cast off, in this respect, *renewing* grace, and is kept from ruin only because of *restraining* grace. He has fallen a great way from grace and returned under the power of the law. Must this not be a great provocation to Christ, that men should cast off His gentle yoke and rule, to cast themselves back under the iron yoke of the law, merely because of their lusts?

Examine yourself also by this: When you are tempted, and must decide whether you will serve sin and rush into folly, like a horse into battle, or fight against it and suppress it, what do you say to your soul? Is it only, 'Hell will be the end of this course; vengeance will meet with me and find me out!' It is time for you to look about you; evil lies at the door. Paul's main argument that sin should not have dominion over believers is that they are 'not under law, but under grace' (*Rom.* 6:14). If your battle against sin is only on legal principles and motives, what assurance do you have that this sin will not have dominion over you, leading to your ruin?

Also, this defence will not last long. If your lust has driven you away from stronger gospel considerations, then considerations of law and penalty will speedily fail you also. These will not restrain you when you have voluntarily given up to your enemy a means of preservation a thousand times stronger. Be sure of this, that unless you recover yourself rapidly from this condition, the thing you fear will come upon you. What *gospel principles* have not done, *legal motives* cannot do!

5. *A fifth dangerous symptom is when it is probable that trouble over a sin or lust is a punishment from God.* I am sure God sometimes leaves even His own children under the power of a particular sin or lust to correct them for former sins. 'O LORD, why do you make us wander from your ways and harden our heart, so that we fear you not?' (*Isa.* 63:17).

No one would question that God deals with unregenerate men in this way, but how can a saved man know if there is the chastening hand of God behind his troubled heart?

Answer: Examine your heart and ways. What was the state of your soul before you fell into the entanglements of the sin now troubling you? Were you negligent in your duties? Were you living without control or self-discipline? Is there the guilt of any great sin lying upon you that you have not repented of? A new sin may be permitted, as well as a new affliction sent, to bring an old sin to remembrance. Have you received any eminent mercy, protection, or deliverance which did not benefit you or for which you were not thankful? Have you experienced any affliction without considering the blessings intended for you behind it? Have you failed to glorify God when He graciously afforded you the opportunity to do so in your generation? Have you been conforming yourself to the world and those in it through the abounding temptations in the day in which you live?

If you have found any of these to be the case with you, awake and call upon God. You are fast asleep with a storm of anger around you!

6. *A sixth dangerous symptom is when your lust has already withstood particular dealings from God against it*. This is described in Isaiah 57:17: 'Because of the iniquity of his unjust gain I was angry. I struck him; I hid my face and was angry, but he went on backsliding in the way of his own heart.'

God had dealt with them about their prevailing lust in several ways, by affliction and desertion; yet they held out against all. This is a sad condition, from which nothing but mere sovereign grace may set a man free, and no-one in such a state should presume upon such deliverance.

God often in His providence meets with a man and speaks particularly of the evil of his heart. He did this to Joseph's brothers for their selling him into Egypt. This makes the man reflect on his sin and judge himself for it. God speaks to a man's heart concerning the danger, affliction, trouble, and sickness that he is in. Sometimes in the reading of the Word, God opens a passage that cuts him to the heart, and shakes him as to his present condition. More frequently, in the hearing of the Word preached, His great ordinance for conviction, conversion, and edification, God strikes with the sword of His Word at the heart of a cherished lust. This startles the sinner and makes him begin to seek the mortification and relinquishment of his heart-evil. Now if his lust has such a strong hold upon him that he seeks to break loose from these constraints, if he allows his lust to stifle conviction, and if he is able to cure his wounds again, he is truly in a sad condition.

This frame of heart is surrounded by countless evils. Every warning a man receives while in this state of mind is a mercy from God. How can he despise God in these mercies by holding out against them? The fact that God does not cast off such a one, and swear in His wrath that he shall never enter into His rest, can only be ascribed to His infinite patience.

These six symptoms, and others with them, show a lust to be very dangerous, if not deadly. Our Saviour said of the evil spirit, 'This kind does not go out but by prayer and fasting.' I would say the same thing about lusts with these symptoms. The ordinary course of mortification will not do. Extraordinary means must be used. The first thing to do then is to consider whether the lust you are fighting has any of these symptoms.

Before I proceed, I must give you one caution so that you will not be misled by what has been said so far. The evils mentioned may ensnare true believers, but do not conclude that because you experience these you are a true believer. These things may *ensnare* a believer, but they are not *marks* of a believer. A man might conclude, with equal show of reasoning, that he is a believer because he is an adulterer, since David fell into adultery. It is wrong to reason that you are a believer because you experience the struggles against sin that a believer also might.

If you are looking for evidences of being a believer, look for those evidences that *constitute* a believer. Anyone who has these serious symptoms may safely conclude, 'If I am a believer, I am a most miserable one.' If such a man is seeking assurance, he needs to look for other evidences in order to have true peace.

10

Seeing Sin for What It Is

PREPARATORY DIRECTION 2: *Get a clear and abiding sense upon your mind and conscience of the guilt, danger, and evil of the sin with which you are troubled.*

1. CONSIDER THE GUILT OF IT. One of the deceptions of a prevailing lust is to play down its guilt, saying, in effect: 'Is it not a little one?'; 'When I bow myself in the house of Rimmon, the LORD pardon your servant in this matter' (*2 Kings* 5:18); 'Though this is bad, yet it is not as bad as such and such an evil, and that which others of the people of God have done! Look what dreadful sins others have fallen into!'

There are many ways in which sin diverts the mind from an appropriate sense of guilt. Sin's loud voice darkens the mind so that it cannot make a right judgment of things. Our perplexing reasonings, our promises calculated to lessen our guilt, turbulent desires, false intentions of reform, and hopes of mercy, all have their part in confusing the mind as it considers the guilt of a prevailing lust.

Hosea tells us that lust in full strength will do all of this: 'Harlotry, and wine and new wine . . . take away the understanding' (*Hos.* 4:11).

This is accomplished to the extreme in unregenerate people, and in part in the regenerate.

Solomon teaches that one who is enticed by the adulteress is 'among the simple', and that he is 'a young man lacking sense' (*Prov.* 7:7). Why does this folly appear? Solomon says in verse 23, 'He does not know that it will cost him his life.' The young man did not consider the guilt of his action. The Lord teaches us that His dealings with Ephraim did not take good effect because he was like a silly dove, without sense (*Hos.* 7:11). Ephraim did not have any understanding of his own miserable condition. Is it possible that King David had lived so long with the guilt of his great sin that his corrupt reasonings hindered him from a clear view of the ugliness and guilt of it? He needed the prophet to awaken him. Through his parable, Nathan broke down David's blindness and self-justification and placed him under the guilt and feeling of his sin. This is the outcome of lust in the heart; it darkens the mind so that it does not rightly judge the guilt of sin.

To help in fixing a right judgment of the guilt of sin in our minds, let us consider the following:

i. For a believer, even though the power of sin is weak-ened by the grace that is in him, and he is not under the authority of sin as others are, the guilt which arises from unmortified sin is aggravated and heightened by the fact that he has received grace.

'What shall we say then? Are we to continue in sin that grace may abound? By no means! How can we who died to sin still live in it?' (*Rom.* 6:1–2). 'How can we who died . . . ?' The emphasis is on the word 'we'. How can *we* do it, who, as he afterwards describes it, have received grace from Christ to the contrary? We, doubtless, are more evil than any if we continue to sin in the light of grace. I shall not insist that the sin itself of such persons is greater than others, even though they sin against more love, mercy, grace, assistance, relief, means, and deliver-ances. But do consider in your mind that the guilt of sinning against grace is more serious than if you did not have any grace at all. Observe also:

ii. God delights in the abundance of beauty and excel-lencies in the hearts of His children more than in the most glorious works of other men. The outward works of fallen man are greatly mixed with sin. The inward desires of grace in the believer are not as greatly mingled with sin. As God sees greater joy in a believer's graces, He also sees a greater evil in the working of their lust and out-ward sins than in the open, notorious acts of wicked men. The outward sins into which the believer may fall are more serious than those of the unsaved, because of the grace opposing them. Thus Christ, in dealing with His failing children, goes to the heart of the matter, sifting actions, as against profession: 'I know your works' (*Rev.* 3:15), as if to say, You are quite another thing than you profess, and this makes you abominable.

Let these considerations, then, give you a clear sense of the guilt of indwelling lust. May there be no room in your heart to justify any sin or lust, or allow it to gain strength and prevail.

2. CONSIDER THE DANGER OF IT, which is manifold:

Danger 1 – Being hardened by the deceitfulness of sin.

'Take care, brothers, lest there be in any of you an evil, unbelieving heart, leading you to fall away from the living God. But exhort one another every day, as long as it is called "today", that none of you may be hardened by the deceitfulness of sin' (*Heb.* 3:12–13).

'Beware', he says, 'use all means, consider your temptations, watch diligently; there is a treachery, a deceit in sin that tends to the hardening of your hearts from the fear of God.' This hardening is so serious that your heart becomes insensitive to moral influence. Sin leads to this. Every sin and lust will make a little progress in this direction. You who at one time were very tender and would melt under the influence of the Word and under trials will grow 'sermon-proof' and 'trial-proof'.

You who used to have great assurance of God's love, trembling at His presence, the thought of death, and your appearance before Him, will now have a hardness in your heart that remains unmoved by these things.

You will have no more conviction in your soul about your sin. You will be able to pass over spiritual duties like prayer, hearing, and reading, with your heart not in the least affected by them. Sin will be a light thing to you and you will not be much troubled about it.

And what will be the end of such a condition? Can a sadder thing happen to you? Is this not enough to make any heart tremble, to think of being in such a state? Alongside of this you will have little thoughts of His grace, of mercy, of the blood of Christ, of the law, and of heaven and hell. Take heed! This is the outcome of harbouring your lust – the hardening of your heart, the searing of your conscience, the blinding of your mind, the dulling of your affections, and the deceiving of your whole soul.

Danger 2 – Coming under a great chastisement.

'If his children forsake my law,
And do not walk according to my rules,
If they violate my statutes,
And do not keep my commandments,
Then I will punish their transgression with the rod,
And their iniquity with stripes' (*Psa.* 89:30–32)

Though God does not utterly cast you off for the abomination that lies in your heart, yet He will visit you with the rod. Even though he will pardon and forgive, He will take vengeance upon your sinful designs. Remember David and all his troubles! Look at him as he flees into the wilderness with the hand of God upon him.

Is it nothing to you that God should kill your child in anger, ruin your estate in anger, break your bones in anger, suffer you to be a scandal and reproach in anger, kill you, destroy you, make you lie down in darkness in anger? Is this nothing to you, that He might punish, ruin, and undo others because of your sin?

Let me not be mistaken. I do not mean that God always sends all these things on His children in anger; God forbid! But this I will say, when He does deal with you in such a way, and your conscience bears witness with Him that you have provoked His judgment, you will find that His dealings will be full of bitterness to your soul. If you do not fear these things, I fear you have been hardened by sin.

Danger 3 – The loss of peace and strength all a man's days.

To have peace with God and strength to walk before Him is the goal of the great promises of the covenant of grace. In these things is the life of our souls. Going on without these, in reasonable abundance, is to die while we live! What good will our lives do us if we do not see the face of God sometimes in peace or do not have a measure of strength to walk with Him? Unmortified lust will deprive us of these blessings. This was the case with David. How often did he complain that his bones were broken, his soul disquieted, his wounds grievous, on this very account!

'Because of the iniquity of his unjust gain I was angry. I struck him; I hid my face and was angry, but he went on backsliding in the way of his own heart' (*Isa.* 57:17).

What peace is there to a soul while God hides Himself? What strength could one have when He strikes?

'I will return again to my place, until they acknowledge their guilt and seek My face' (*Hos.* 5:15); as if to say, 'I will leave them, hide my face, and what will become of their peace and strength?'

If you have ever enjoyed peace with God, if ever His terrors have made you afraid, if you have ever enjoyed strength to walk with Him, if you have ever mourned in your prayers, or if you have been troubled because of your weakness, then think of the dangers that hang over your head!

It may only be a little while and you shall see the face of God in peace no more. Perhaps by tomorrow you shall not be able to pray, read, hear, or perform any duties with the least cheerfulness, life, or vigour. Perhaps you may never see a quiet hour while you live and you will carry broken bones about you, full of pain and terror all the days of your life. Perhaps God will shoot his arrows at you and fill you with anguish and uneasiness, with fears and perplexities, and make you a terror and astonishment to yourself and others. Perhaps He will show you hell and wrath every moment, frighten and scare you with sad apprehensions of His hatred, so that your wound shall afflict you by night and your soul refuse to have comfort. You will wish for death rather than life.

Though God should not utterly destroy you, yet He might cast you into this condition to give you a sharp and living apprehension of your destruction. Consider in your heart the terrible outcome of such a state. Do not stop thinking about it till your soul trembles within you.

Danger 4 – The danger of eternal destruction.

To rightly understand this, consider two things:

First, there is a connection between continuing in sin and eternal destruction. God does graciously deliver some from continuing in sin so that they may not be destroyed. However, He will not deliver any from destruction that do indeed continue in sin! For any that lie under the abiding power of sin, the threats of destruction and everlasting separation from God should be held out (*Heb.* 3:12; 10:38). This is the rule of God's proceeding – if any man 'departs' from Him, 'shrinks back' through unbelief, God's 'soul has no pleasure in him'; that is, God's indignation shall pursue him to destruction (*Gal.* 6:8).

Secondly, he that is so entangled, as described above, is under the power of corruption, and has no clear evidence of participating in the grace of God. Such a one cannot claim any assurance that he is delivered from destruction. Destruction from the Lord should be an appropriate fear for him. Such a one should seriously consider this to be the end of his course and ways. 'There is . . . no condemnation for those who are in Christ Jesus' (*Rom.* 8:1). True, but who shall have the comfort of this promise? Who can claim it for themselves? Those who 'walk not according to the flesh but according to the Spirit' (*Rom.* 8:4).

But you will say, 'Does this not lead people away from faith?' I answer, No. Whatever evidence we may have of our own salvation, we must acknowledge that an evil path leads to destruction. To believe otherwise is atheism. We are not throwing away the good evidence of a personal interest in Christ, but an evil path throws doubt upon the reality of it. We should surely fly from a path that leads to death! The realization that the end of such a path is destruction should move us to free ourselves from the entanglement of our lusts.

3. CONSIDER THE PRESENT EVILS OF IT. Here are some of the many evils that attend unmortified lust:

i. *It grieves the holy and blessed Spirit,* Who is given to believers to dwell in them and abide with them. Paul, after exhorting the Ephesians to turn away from many lusts and sins gives this as the great motive of it: 'Do not grieve the Holy Spirit of God, by whom you were sealed for the day of redemption' (*Eph.* 4:30).

That is, do not grieve the indwelling One from whom we have received so many and great blessings, especially the keeping of our souls till the day of redemption! He is grieved by our sin as a tender and loving friend is grieved by wounds from a close friend. The Holy Spirit has chosen our hearts for a dwelling place, and He is there to do for us all that our souls desire. He is therefore grieved by our harbouring His enemies, and that which He is seeking to destroy in our hearts.

'He does not afflict willingly or grieve the children of men' (*Lam.* 3:33). Shall we then daily grieve Him? If there is any gracious character in our soul, if it is not entirely hardened by the deceitfulness of sin, then *not grieving the Spirit* is surely a great motive for purity. Consider who you are, and who the Spirit is whom you are grieving. Consider what He has done for you already and be ashamed! Among those who walk with God, there is no greater motive and incentive to universal holiness, and the preserving of our hearts and spirits in all purity and cleanness, than this, that we keep our hearts undefiled for the blessed Spirit Who dwells in us as the temple of God, and keeps us for the Lord. Zimri aggravated his sin when he displayed it in the sight of Moses and the rest (*Num.* 25:6). Is it not also a serious aggravation of the guilt of our sin when it is (as it must be, if we are believers) performed under the eye of the Holy Spirit who desires His dwelling place to be pure and holy?

ii. *The Lord Jesus Christ is wounded afresh by it.* His new creation in the heart is wounded; His love is foiled; His adversary is gratified. If deceitful sin engulfs the will, crucifies again the Son of God, and puts Him to open shame (*Heb.* 6:6), so every harbouring of sin that He came to destroy wounds and grieves Him.

iii. *It will take away a man's usefulness in his generation.* His works, his endeavours, his labours, will seldom receive blessing from God. He labours as though in the fire, without any success in his work. The world is full of poor professors without reality. How few are there that walk in beauty and glory! How barren, and how useless are they for the most part! Among the many reasons that may be assigned for this sad state is the harbouring of spirit-devouring lusts in one's bosom. Sin lies as a worm at the root of obedience and corrodes and weakens it day by day. All graces, ways and means whereby one might be improved are hindered by sin. God blasts such men's efforts.

Thus, we must keep in mind the danger of such lust. We must keep alive in our hearts the guilt, danger and evil of it. We should be much in the meditation of these things, and cause the heart and mind to dwell on them. We should engage our thoughts in these considerations. We should not let them go from us until they have a powerful influence upon our souls, and make us tremble.

11

A Tender Conscience and a Watchful Heart

PREPARATORY DIRECTION 3: *Charge your conscience with the guilt of indwelling sin.* Not only should you acknowledge that it brings guilt upon you, but you should charge your conscience with the guilt of its actual risings and out-breakings.

I shall develop this direction with some more specific instructions.

First, *let us consider indwelling sin in relation to the law of God.*

Allow the guilt displayed in the holy law to speak to your conscience. Lay your particular corruption next to the law and let its pressure weigh heavily on your conscience. Consider the law in its holiness, spirituality, severity, and see if you can stand before it in your corruption. Allow the terror of the Lord as displayed in the law to affect you greatly. Consider how righteous it is that every one of your transgressions should receive a just reward of judgment. Perhaps your conscience might seek to escape the ramifications of this line of reasoning. You might say that you are not under the condemning power of the law and that you have been freed from it. There is therefore no need to be troubled by it. But,

i. Tell your conscience that it cannot be assured that you are free from the condemning power of sin while your unmortified lust dwells in your heart. Perhaps the law has full dominion over you and you are indeed a lost creature! It is best to consider seriously what the law has to say.

Assuredly, he that pleads in the deepest part of his heart that he is truly freed from the condemning power of the law, and yet purposely allows the least sin or lust to be entertained there, cannot upon gospel authority have any proof of spiritual security. How can he consider himself truly delivered from the very sin that he is entertaining?

ii. The law was commissioned by God to judge sin wherever it finds it, and bring it before His throne. Here you stand before God and His law has found you out and is condemning your sin. If you can plead pardon, that will be well and good, but if not, the law will do its work and you will be condemned.

iii. The purpose of the law is to discover sin and the guilt of it. It should awaken and humble the soul and reveal sin in all of its horrible colours. If you are unwilling to deal with it on this account, this is an indication of a hard heart under the deceitfulness of sin. This is a door that many professing believers have entered, which has led them into open apostasy. They have claimed deliverance from the law so that they might ignore its guidance and direction. They do not want to measure their sin by the law any more. Little by little this attitude influences their daily lives, and allows their will and affections to run to all manner of abominations.

It is important, then, for your conscience to pay attention to the law as it speaks concerning your lust and corruption. If your ears are open, the law will speak with a voice that will make you tremble. The law will cast you to the ground and fill you with astonishment. If you intend ever to gain the victory in mortification, you must tie your conscience to the law. Do not allow it to dodge the law's arrows. Allow the law to give you a clear view of your guilt. As King David says, 'My sin is ever before me' (*Psa.* 51:3).

Secondly, *let us consider sin in relation to the gospel.*
Bring your lust to the gospel. Not for relief, but for further conviction of your guilt. Look on Him whom you have pierced, and let it trouble you. Say to your soul, 'What have I done? What love, what mercy, what blood, what grace have I despised and trampled on! Is this how

I pay back the Father for His love? Is this how I thank the Son for His blood? Is this how I respond to the Holy Spirit for His grace? Have I defiled the heart that Christ died to wash, and the Holy Spirit has chosen to dwell in? How can I keep myself out of the dust? What can I say to the dear Lord Jesus? How shall I hold up my head with any boldness before Him? Do I count fellowship with Him of so little value that, for this vile lust's sake, I have hardly left Him any room in my heart? How shall I escape if I neglect so great salvation?

'What shall I say to the Lord? His love, mercy, grace, goodness, peace, joy, consolation – I have despised all of them! I have considered them as nothing, that I might harbour lust in my heart. Have I seen God as my Father, that I might provoke Him to His face? Was my soul washed that there might be room for new defilements? Shall I seek to disappoint the purpose of the death of Christ? Shall I grieve the Holy Spirit, Who has sealed me unto the day of redemption?' Allow your conscience to consider these things every day. See if your conscience can resist the way in which these considerations aggravate guilt. If this does not cause your conscience to sink and melt, I fear that your case is very dangerous.

Then let us consider three particular instructions.

1. We should love and consider all the benefits we have under the gospel. As we cherish our redemption, justification and the like, certainly this will aggravate the guilt of the corruptions of our hearts.

1. *Consider the infinite patience and forbearance of God towards us.* Consider how He might have been against you and made you a shame and reproach in the world. You might have been an object of wrath forever. How you have dealt treacherously and falsely with Him from time to time. You have flattered Him with your lips, while breaking all promises and engagements by holding to the sin you are now seeking. He has spared you from time to time and you have tested Him to see how long He might be patient. Will you continue to sin against Him? Will you weary Him and cause Him to put up with your corruptions?

Have you not often felt that it seemed impossible that He could bear much longer with you? That He might cast you off, and be gracious no more? That all His forbearance was exhausted, and that hell and wrath were now prepared for you? Yet, despite this expectation, He has returned with visitations of love. Will you yet abide in that which provokes the eyes of His glory?

2. *How many times have you been at the door of being hardened by sin, and then the infinite and rich grace of God has recovered you to fellowship with Him again?* Have you not found yourself slipping from the delights of your spiritual duties? Has your desire for the ordinances, prayer, and meditation begun to vanish? Has the inclination to a loose and careless walk before God begun to thrive? It is amazing that this might happen to those who have been rescued from entanglements almost beyond

recovery! Are you finding yourself delightfully engaged in such ways and friendships as are a grief to the Lord? Will you allow yourself to drift any further towards the brink of hardness of heart?

3. *It is important now to consider all God's gracious dealings with you.* Consider His providential blessings, deliverances, mercies, and enjoyments that He has given you. Fill your conscience with such memories. Do not leave these meditations until your heart is strongly influenced with the guilt of indwelling corruption.

Continue with such meditations until you feel the wound of your corruptions in your conscience and you seek to lie in the dust before the Lord. Unless you can get your conscience into such a state, you will not be able to gain the victory. As long as your conscience is able to justify your failure, your soul will never vigorously attempt the mortification of sin.

PREPARATORY DIRECTION 4: *Seek a constant longing and thirsting to be delivered from the power of sin.* Do not let your heart be happy with your present condition, even for a moment.

In natural and civil matters, the desire for change is of no value unless it stirs up a person to use the means leading to the desired end. It is different, however, in spiritual things. The desire, longing, and panting after deliverance is in itself a grace which begins to conform the soul to the likeness of that which is longed for.

The apostle Paul considers the repentance and sorrow of the Corinthians as a work of grace (2 *Cor.* 7:11). In his own case, in Romans 7:24, Paul's heart breaks forth with a passionate expression of the desire to be delivered from the power of sin. If this is a Christian's frame of mind concerning the general state of indwelling sin, should not the desire for deliverance be magnified when you add to this the guilt of a particular lust or corruption! Be assured, unless you long for deliverance you will not find it.

Your longing heart will now watch for all opportunities to gain an advantage over its enemy. It will readily fall in with all the help it can find to accomplish sin's destruction. A strong desire is the life-blood of praying without ceasing! A strong desire sets faith and hope to work, and drives the soul in following hard after the Lord. Get your heart into a strong longing and panting attitude. Long for, and cry out for, righteousness. Remember the example of David: 'O God, you are my God; earnestly I seek you' (*Psa.* 63:1).

PREPARATORY DIRECTION 5: *Consider whether the trouble that you are perplexed with is related to your particular make-up and nature.* Does your personal constitution heighten and cherish some particular sin? A proneness to some sins may doubtless lie in the natural temper and disposition of individuals. In such a case let us consider three things:

1. This is <u>not in the least a just excuse</u> for the guilt of your sin. Some with an open irreverence ascribe gross, abnormal tendencies to their make-up. It may even be that others deny their own guilt for sin by the same consideration. It is from the Fall and the original depravity of our nature that the poison and nourishment of any sin abides in our natural temper. David considered his being formed in sin (*Psa.* 51:5) as a further aggravation of his transgression, and not a lessening of it. If you are particularly inclined to any particular sinful action, it is but the breaking out of original lust in your nature, and this should humble you.

2. If your constitution is particularly prone to give way to a particular lust, then Satan and sin have a special advantage, and you must, with extraordinary watchfulness, care, and diligence, fight to overcome these attacks against your soul. Thousands have been on this account hurried headlong to hell, who might otherwise at least have gone at a more gentle, less provoking, and less mischievous rate.

3. For the mortification of any sin so rooted in the nature of a man, there is one expedient particularly suited for him: 'I discipline my body and keep it under control' (*1 Cor.* 9:27). Bringing the body into subjection can indeed assist in mortification. Perhaps because of the papists who, in ignorance of the righteousness of Christ and the work of His Spirit, have emphasized services and

penances without the knowledge of the true nature of sin and mortification, others might neglect this kind of means as appropriate. But bringing the body into subjection by cutting short the natural appetite, by fasting, watching and the like, are doubtless acceptable to God and may be done, subject to the following guidelines:

i. The outward weakening and impairing of the body should not be looked upon as a good thing in itself. This would make us subject to fleshly ordinances which are not true mortification. A man can have leanness of body and leanness of soul together. Bringing the body into subjection is a benefit only as it leads to the weakening of sin in its root and seat.

ii. Fasting and watching and the like should not be looked upon as things which in themselves have the ability to produce true mortification. If they were able to do this, sin might be mortified without any help of the Spirit by any unregenerate person in the world. These disciplines are to be looked upon only as means by which the Spirit may, and sometimes does, put forth strength for the accomplishing of His own work.

PREPARATORY DIRECTION 6: *Consider what occasions your sin has taken advantage of to exert itself in the past, and watch carefully at such times.* This is one part of the duty that our blessed Saviour recommends to his disciples: 'What I say to you, I say to all: Stay awake' (*Mark* 13:37). Also, 'Watch yourselves lest your hearts be weighed down with dissipation' (*Luke* 21:34).

We need to watch against every breaking out of our corruptions. David said, 'I kept myself from my guilt' (*Psa.* 18:23). He watched all the ways and workings of his iniquity, to prevent them, and to rise up against them. This is what we are called to do by Scripture when it says, 'Consider your ways' (*Hag.* 1:5)!

Consider what ways, what kinds of company, what opportunities, what studies, what occupations, what conditions have at any time given, or do usually give, advantages to your sins, and set yourself against them all. Men will do this with their bodily infirmities. The season, the diet and the air that have proved offensive are avoided. Are the things of the soul of less importance? If we dare to dally with the occasions of sin, we will dare to sin. He that will venture on the temptation to wickedness will venture on wickedness itself. Hazael did not think he would ever be as wicked as the prophet said he would be (*2 Kings* 8:13). However, if a man will venture on the temptation to be cruel, he will be cruel! You might tell a man that he will commit such and such sins and he might be surprised. But if he is willing to venture upon the occasions that lead to these sins, he has little ground left for his confidence.

PREPARATORY DIRECTION 7: *Rise mightily against the first sign of sin*. Do not allow it to gain the smallest ground. Do not say 'Thus far I shall go, and no farther.' If you allow it one step, it will take another. It is impossible to fix boundaries for sin! It is like water in a channel. If it

[85]

ever breaks out, it will flow on through the breach. It is easier to stop it in the beginning than after it has begun to run.

James teaches that sin is progressive (*James* 1:14–15). Do you find corruption beginning to entangle your thoughts? Rise up with all of your strength against it, as if it had already started to overcome you. Consider what an unclean thought desires. It desires to have you immerse yourself in folly and filth.

Ask envy what it aims at. Murder and destruction are its natural conclusion. Set yourself against it as if it had already surrounded you in wickedness. If you do not in this way attack temptation, you will not win the battle. If sin gains ground in your affections so that you delight in it, your understanding will also come to think little of it.

12

Humility

PREPARATORY DIRECTION 8: *We need to be exercised with such meditations as will fill us at all times with self-abasement and thoughts of our own vileness.*

1. Meditate upon the excellence and the majesty of God and our infinite, inconceivable distance from Him. These meditations will fill us with our own vileness and strike deep at the root of our indwelling sin. When Job discovered God's greatness and majesty it filled him with self-abhorrence and humility (*Job* 42:5-6). Notice how Habakkuk felt when he was made aware of the glory and majesty of God:

'I hear, and my body trembles;
My lips quiver at the sound;

Rottenness enters into my bones;
My legs tremble beneath me' (*Hab*. 3:16).

'God is clothed', says Job, 'with awesome majesty' (*Job* 37:22).

Such were the thoughts of men of old. When they saw God, they thought they would die. The Scriptures abound in these self-abasing considerations. Men of the earth are compared to 'grasshoppers', to 'vanity', and 'dust on the scales', in respect to God (*Isa*. 40:12–25).

Consider these things often to abase the pride of your heart and to keep your soul humble within you. Such a frame of heart will be a great advantage in conquering the deceitfulness of sin. Think often of the greatness of God.

2. Consider often how unacquainted you really are with God. Certainly you know enough to keep you low and humble, but how little we really know of Him!

In such consideration the wise may speak as Agur:

'Surely I am too stupid to be a man. I have not the understanding of a man. I have not learned wisdom, nor have I knowledge of the Holy One. Who has ascended to heaven and come down? Who has gathered the wind in his fists? Who has wrapped up the waters in a garment? Who has established all the ends of the earth? What is His name, and what is His Son's name? Surely you know!' (*Prov*. 30:2–4).

Labour to limit your pride with these considerations:

What do you know about God? How little a portion of His majesty! How immense He is in His nature! Can you look without terror into the abyss of eternity? Can you bear the rays of His glorious Being?

I consider these meditations of great value in our walking with God, so far as they are consistent with our filial boldness in seeking Him at the throne of grace through our Lord Jesus Christ. These thoughts should leave an abiding impression on the souls of those who desire to walk humbly with God.

Seek to keep your heart in a continual awe of the majesty of God. Realize that the most learned and eminent, and the nearest and most familiar in communion with God, still in this life, know but very little of Him and His glory. To Moses was revealed the most glorious attributes that He can reveal in the covenant of grace (*Exod.* 34:5–6), but even these are but the 'back parts' of God!

All that Moses saw and learned was but little compared with the perfections of God's glory. It is with peculiar reference to Moses that John said, 'No one has ever seen God' (*John* 1:18). John was speaking of the Father in comparison with the Son. It is said of the Father, 'No one', no, not even Moses, the most eminent among them, 'has ever seen God.' We may speak much of God; talk of Him, His ways, His works, His counsels, all day long; but the truth is, we know very little of Him. Our thoughts, our meditations, our expressions of Him are low, many of them unworthy of His glory, and none of them reaching His perfections.

One might argue that Moses was under the law and wrapped in the darkness of types and shadowy institutions, but that now, under the glorious shining of the gospel, in which God has brought life and immortality to light, we see Him much more clearly. Now we see Him as He is, and now also His face, not like Moses, who only saw His 'back parts'.

Answer 1

I acknowledge that there is a vast and almost inconceivable difference between what we now know, after God has spoken in the Son, and what was known by the saints under the law. Even though their eyes were as good, sharp and clear as ours, and their faith and spiritual understanding not at all behind ours, the object of their faith was as glorious to them as to us, yet our day is more clear than theirs was! The clouds are blown away and scattered. The shadows of the night are gone and fled away. The sun has risen, and the means of sight is made more eminent and clear than formerly. But then,

Answer 2

That peculiar sight which Moses had of God (*Exod.* 34), was a gospel-sight, a sight of God as 'gracious', etc., and yet it is called but His 'back parts', that is, but low and inferior, in comparison with His excellencies and perfections. Also,

Answer 3

The apostle Paul exalts the gospel light above that of the law, saying that the veil causing darkness is taken away and we now see with an unveiled face the glory of the Lord (*2 Cor.* 3:18). But how does he say that we see it? As in a mirror! How is that? Clearly, or perfectly? Alas, no! He tells us that we see in a mirror, dimly! (*1 Cor.* 13:12). How short do we come of the truth of things. We are looking in a looking glass where we see only obscure images of things, and not the things themselves! This is how he assesses our knowledge. We see by or through this glass. It is in darkness and obscurity. Paul, speaking of himself, who was much more clear-sighted than any now living, tells us that he saw 'in part'. He saw but the back parts of heavenly things, and compares all the knowledge he has attained of God to the knowledge of a child (*1 Cor.* 13:11).

We know about the weak and uncertain understandings of children. When they grow up, these vanish away. It is right for a child to love, honour, believe, and obey his father; and yet his father is aware of his childhood weaknesses. We are like children. Notwithstanding all our confidence of high attainments, all our notions of God are but childish with regard to His infinite perfections. We lisp and babble in our most accurate, as we think, understandings of God. We may love, honour, believe, and obey our Father; and in this our faith He accepts our childishness. We see only His back parts. We know little of Him. We thus appreciate that promise which often supports and comforts us in our distress: 'We shall see Him as He is', we shall see Him 'face to face', and, 'Then I shall know fully, even as I have been fully known' (*1 Cor.* 13:12; *1 John* 3:2)

Now, we do not see Him fully, but in a dark, obscure representation. We do not see the perfection of His glory.

The queen of Sheba had heard much of Solomon, and formed great thoughts of his magnificence in her mind. But when she came and saw his glory, she was forced to confess that not half the truth had been told her.

We may suppose that we have here attained great knowledge, clear and high thoughts of God, but, alas! When He shall bring us into His presence we shall cry out, 'We never knew Him as He is; only a thousandth of His glory, and perfection, and blessedness, has ever entered our hearts!'

The apostle John tells us in 1 John 3:2 that we do not know what we ourselves shall be in that day, much less can we conceive now what God is, and what we shall find Him to be in eternity.

Let us further consider who it is that we seek to know:

First, we know so little of God because it is *God* we are seeking to know. God Himself has revealed Himself as one who cannot be known. He calls Himself invisible, incomprehensible, and the like. We cannot fully know Him as He is. Our progress often consists more in knowing what He is not, than what He is. He is immortal and infinite and we are only mortal, finite, and limited.

'Who alone has immortality, who dwells in unapproachable light, whom no one has ever seen or can see. To him be honour and eternal dominion. Amen' (*1 Tim.* 6:16).

His light is such that no creature can approach Him. He is not seen, not because He cannot be seen, but because we cannot bear the sight of Him. The light of God, in Whom is no darkness, forbids all access to Him by any creature. We who cannot behold the sun in its glory are too weak to bear the beams of infinite brightness. In considering the glory of God, Agur (*Prov.* 30:2) considered himself more stupid than any man, and not even having the understanding of a man. He knew nothing in comparison with God; so that he seemed to have lost all his understanding when he came to the consideration of God, His work, and His ways.

In this consideration, let us weigh two particulars:

i. When we consider *the very being of God*, we find ourselves so far from the true knowledge of it that we cannot come up with the right words and expressions. As we seek to meditate in our minds and frame thoughts about God as we do about other objects of thinking, we fall so far short that we make an idol in our mind and worship a god of our own making, and not the true God that has made us. We may as well hew him out of wood or stone as form him as a being in our minds, suited to our imaginations. The best thoughts of the being of God are ones in which we realize that we cannot truly comprehend Him as He is. We realize that we know so little when our best thoughts of God are, 'We cannot know.'

ii. There are some truths of God that He has taught us to speak of. He has even guided us in our expressions of them. But when we have done so *we do not really fully understand* these things. All we can do is believe and admire. We profess, as we are taught that God is infinite, omnipotent, eternal; and we know the discussions about His omnipresence, immensity, infinity and eternity. We have, I say, words and notions about these things; but as to the things themselves, what do we really know? What do we comprehend of them? Can the mind of man do any more than be swallowed up in an infinite abyss and give itself up to what it cannot conceive or express? Is not our understanding 'brutish' in the contemplation of such things?

We are more perfect in our understanding when we realize that we cannot understand, and rest there. It is just the back parts of eternity and infinity that we see. What shall we say of the Trinity, or the existence of three Persons in the same individual essence? This is such a mystery that it is denied by many, because they cannot understand it. Is it not indeed a mystery whose every letter is mysterious? Who can declare the generation of the Son, the procession of the Spirit, or the difference of the one from the other? Thus, the infinite and inconceivable distance that is between Him and us keeps us in the dark as to any sight of His face or clear apprehension of His perfections.

We know Him rather by what He does than by what He is. We understand His doing us good, but not truly His essential goodness. How little a portion of Him, as Job says, is discovered in this way!

Secondly, we know little of God because it is *by faith alone and not by actual sight* that we know God while on earth. All men have impressions in their hearts that there is a God. Their reason so teaches them, through the works of His creation and providence. Their understanding, however, as has been seen by experience in all the ages before, is weak, low, dark, and confused. Man on this account has not glorified God as he should and, notwithstanding all this knowledge of God, man is without God in the world.

The chief and almost only acquaintance we have with God is by faith. 'Whoever would draw near to God must believe that He exists, and that he rewards those who seek Him' (*Heb.* 11:6). 'We walk by faith, not by sight' (*2 Cor.* 5:7).

Faith is the only argument we have of things 'not seen' (*Heb.* 11:1). Since it is by faith alone that we have true knowledge of God, we only see the back parts of His reality. As to the beginning of our faith, it is built upon the testimony of the One we have not seen! We love Him though we have not seen Him (*1 Pet.* 1:8). Our faith rests solely on His testimony and not upon some outward manifestation of evidence. The object of our faith is beyond our ability to grasp fully. Our faith then is 'seeing dimly, as in a mirror'. Thus all that we know is low, dark and obscure.

But someone may say: All this is true for unbelievers, but with those who have trusted in Christ it is different! For, 'No man has seen God at any time', but, 'the only begotten Son, which is in the bosom of the Father, he has declared him' (*John* 1:18, AV); and, 'The Son of God has come and has given us understanding, so that we may know him who is true' (*1 John* 5:20); and the illumination of 'the gospel of the glory of Christ, who is the image of God' shines upon believers (*2 Cor.* 4:4). Yes, and 'God, who said, "Let light shine out of darkness", has shone in our hearts, to give the light of the knowledge of his glory in the face of Jesus Christ' (*2 Cor.* 4:6). So that though we were 'darkness', yet we are now 'light in the Lord' (*Eph.* 5:8). And the apostle says, 'We all, with unveiled face, behold the glory of the Lord' (*2 Cor.* 3:18).

We are now very far from being in such darkness, or at such a distance from God. 'Our fellowship is with the Father and with His Son' (*1 John* 1:3). The light of the gospel, which God has revealed to us, is not a star, but the Sun. His beauty is risen upon us and the veil is taken away from our faces! Unbelievers and perhaps some weak believers may yet be in some darkness, but those of any growth or considerable attainments have a clear sight and view of the face of God in Jesus Christ.

To which I answer:

i. The truth is that we all know enough of Him to love Him more than we do, to delight in Him and serve Him, to believe Him and obey Him, and to put our trust in Him much beyond our current attainments. Our darkness and weakness is no excuse for our negligence and disobedience. Who can say that he has lived up to the knowledge that he has of the perfections, excellencies and will of God?

God's purpose in giving us any knowledge of Himself is that we may glorify Him as God. That is, that we love Him, serve Him, believe and obey Him, and give Him all the honour and glory that is due from such poor sinful creatures to a sin-pardoning God and Creator. But we must all acknowledge that we have never thoroughly been transformed into the image of the knowledge that we have. If we had used our talents better, we might have been trusted with more.

ii. The knowledge we have of God through the revelation of Christ Jesus is exceedingly eminent and glorious. It is superior when compared with any other knowledge of God we might have attained, such as was delivered under the Old Testament. The Old Testament was a shadow of the good things to come (*2 Cor.* 3). Christ has now in these last days revealed the Father from His own bosom, declared His Name, and made known His mind and will. His counsels are far more clear, eminent, and distinct in manner than they were formerly while His people were under the authority of the Law. The scriptures mentioned mostly had this in mind. The clear and transparent declaration of God and His will as seen in the gospel is expressly exalted in comparison with any other way He has revealed Himself.

iii. The difference between believers and unbelievers as to knowledge is not so much in the *matter* of their knowledge, as in the *manner* of their knowing. Unbelievers, some of them, may know more and be able to say more of God, His perfections, and His will, than many believers; but they do not know God as they should. They do not know in the right manner; their knowledge is not spiritual and saving, and it does not have a heavenly light. The excellence of a believer is not that he has a large apprehension of things, but that what he does understand, which may be very little, he sees in the light of the Spirit of God. He has a saving, soul-transforming light. This is what gives us communion with God.

iv. Jesus Christ by His Word and Spirit reveals to His own that God is our heavenly Father and our Rewarder. He teaches us sufficiently how to obey Him now and how to know intimate fellowship with Him now and to eternity. But yet,

v. Notwithstanding all this, it is but a little portion we know of Him. We only see His back parts. For,

First, the purpose of all gospel revelation is not to unveil God in His essential glory that we might see him in the fullness of Who He is. The gospel only declares so much of Him as is sufficient to be the foundation of our faith, love, obedience and coming to Him. We have enough knowledge to exercise the faith He expects from us here, and sufficient resources for the victory of poor creatures in the midst of temptations. But when He calls us to heaven, where we will be admitted to eternal admiration and contemplation without interruption, He will reveal Himself in a greater way, with the full manifestation of His glory.

Secondly, we are dull and slow of heart to receive the things that are revealed in His Word. God uses our infirmity and weakness to keep us in continual dependence on Him for teachings and revelations of Himself out of His Word. Though we do understand the revelation in the gospel clearly, He never in this world brings any soul to the full knowledge of all in His Word that might be discovered.

Will not a due apprehension of the inconceivable greatness of God, and the infinite distance in which we stand from Him, fill our souls with a holy and awful fear of Him, and keep us in a frame unsuited for the thriving and flourishing of any lust whatever. We should continually be accustomed to reverential thoughts of God's greatness and omnipresence. Then we will always be watchful against any behaviour not suited to His presence.

Consider Him with whom we are dealing: 'Our God is a consuming fire' (*Heb*. 12:29). And, as we stand abashed in His presence, let us realize that our very nature is too limited to have an adequate sense of His essential glory.

13

Wait for the
Verdict of God

PREPARATORY DIRECTION 9: *When God stirs your heart about the guilt of your sin, concerning either its root and indwelling, or its breaking out, be careful you do not speak peace to yourself before God speaks it. Listen closely to what He says to your soul.*

Without careful observation of this direction, your heart will be very exposed to the deceitfulness of sin.

This is a business of great importance. It is a sad thing for a man to deceive his own soul in this way. All the warnings God gives us, in tenderness to our souls, to examine ourselves, are to prevent this great evil of speaking peace to ourselves without due warrant. This is to bless ourselves, without the blessing of God.

How can we prevent this? First, two observations.

Observation 1: It is the great prerogative of God in His sovereignty to give grace to whom He pleases. 'He has mercy on whom He wills' (*Rom.* 9:18).

Among all the sons of men, He calls whom He wills, and sanctifies whom He wills. Among those so called and sanctified, He yet reserves this privilege to Himself also, to speak peace to whom He pleases, and in what degree he pleases, even among them on whom He has bestowed grace. He is the 'God of all comfort' in a special manner in His dealings with believers. God keeps good things locked up for his family, and gives them out to all His children at His pleasure.

In Isaiah 57:16–18 God says He will heal their brokenness and misery, and He assumes this privilege to Himself in a special way: 'Creating the fruit of the lips: Peace, peace, to the far and to the near, says the LORD, and I will heal him' (*Isa.* 57:19).

In the display of grace to the world, God works in a mystery. In His taking and leaving, as to outward appearances, His ways are often contrary to all probable expectations. So, in His communication of peace and joy to those in a state of grace, He often acts in a way that confounds our expectations.

Observation 2: Just as God creates peace for whom he pleases, so it is the prerogative of Christ to apply it to the conscience. Speaking to the church of Laodicea, which had healed her wounds falsely and spoken peace to herself when she should not have, He takes to himself that title, 'I am the Amen, the faithful and true witness'(*Rev.* 3:14).

He bears testimony to our condition in truth. We may be mistaken and trouble ourselves in vain, or flatter ourselves upon false grounds, but He is the 'Amen, the faithful and true witness', and what He speaks of our state and condition, that it is indeed!

Secondly, with these two observations in mind, I shall give five rules by which men may know whether God speaks peace to them or whether they speak peace to themselves only.

Rule 1: Men certainly speak peace to themselves when they do not view their sin, from the guilt of which they seek relief, with the greatest hatred imaginable. There should be an abhorrence of themselves for that sin.

If men are wounded by sin, disturbed and perplexed, and realize that there is no remedy for them except in the mercy of God and through the blood of Christ; and if such look to Him and His covenant promises, and upon this basis quiet their hearts, believing that it will indeed be well with them, and that God will be gracious to them – and yet they do not detest with utter hatred the sin in question – this is to heal themselves and not to be healed by God. This is like the great and strong wind that the Lord was near to, but the Lord was not in the wind

(*1 Kings* 19:11)! When a man truly looks upon Christ whom he has pierced, without whom there is no healing or peace, and mourns (*Zech.* 12:10), his mourning will be because it was his sin that pierced Him!

When we go to Christ for healing, our faith sees Him particularly as the one pierced. Our faith views Him in different ways, just as the reasons for which we seek communion with Him differ. Sometimes we view His holiness, sometimes His power, sometimes His love, and sometimes His favour with His Father. But when we come for healing and peace our faith looks especially to the blood of the covenant and to His sufferings, for, 'with his stripes we are healed', and 'upon him was the chastisement that brought us peace' (*Isa.* 53:5).

When we come for healing, we consider His stripes – not in the physical sense, but with respect to the love, kindness, mystery, and design of the cross. When we look for peace His chastisements come before our minds.

Now if this is done according to the mind of God, and in the strength of the Holy Spirit, who is poured out on believers, it will cause a hatred of the sin or sins on account of which healing and peace are sought. 'Yet I will remember my covenant with you in the days of your youth, and I will establish for you an everlasting covenant.' And what then? 'Then you will remember your ways and be ashamed' (*Ezek.* 16:60–61).

When God comes to us and speaks peace to us, He fills our soul with shame for all the ways in which we have been alienated from Him. And one of the things that the apostle mentions as attending the Corinthians' repentance over their failures was indignation for their own folly (*2 Cor.* 7:11).

When Job arrived at a thorough healing, he cried; 'Therefore I despise myself' (*Job* 42:6). Until he had done so, he did not have abiding peace. He might have rested in Elihu's message of free grace (*Job* 33:14-30), but that would not have healed his wounds completely. He had to abhor himself if he was to have a full recovery.

How different it was with those in Psalm 78:33–35. They were in great trouble and perplexity on account of their sin. They called upon God as their Rock and their Redeemer, which certainly was a type of looking to Christ. They spoke peace thus to themselves, but it was not abiding! No, it passed away as the early dew. God did not speak one word of peace to their souls. Why did they not experience peace? Because in their prayers to God they flattered Him. How does that appear? Verse 37: 'Their heart was not steadfast towards him; they were not faithful to his covenant.' They did not hate nor relinquish the sin on account of which they were seeking peace for themselves.

Let a man seek as he will for healing and peace, let him go to the true Physician, let him seek in the right way and let him quiet his heart in the promises of the covenant. Yet when peace is spoken, if it is not attended with hatred and abhorrence of the sin which caused the wound and was the reason for all the trouble, then this is not God's peace, but a peace of our own making.

It is but a covering over the wound, while the infection underneath continues to fester, corrupt and corrode, until it breaks out again with greater foulness, vexation and danger.

Let not the poor souls that walk in this path ever think that they will have true and solid peace. They are more concerned with the trouble of the sin than the pollution and uncleanness that accompanies it. They call to the Lord Jesus Christ for mercy, but they still keep the sweet morsel of sin under their tongue!

If you are dealing with God in Christ for the healing of your soul and the quieting of your conscience, but you do not have a thorough hatred of your sin, perhaps you may be saved, yet it will be as through fire. Perhaps you like the sin well enough, but only dislike the consequences of it. God will work further with you before He is done, but you will have little peace in this life; you will be sick and fainting all your days (*Isa.* 57:17).

This is a deceit that lies at the root of the peace of many professors, but it ruins that peace. They expend great energy to obtain mercy and pardon. They seem to have great communion with God in their so doing. They lie before him and bewail their sins and follies.

One might think, indeed, they think themselves, that surely they and their sins are now pardoned. This satisfies their hearts for a little season. But when a thorough search is made, there has been some secret provision made for that same folly! At least, there has not been that thorough hatred of sin that was necessary. Soon their peace is discovered to be weak and rotten. It does not last much beyond the words of pleading that came out of their mouths.

Rule 2: Men also speak peace to themselves when they reason from the gracious promises of God and claim them in a purely rational and natural way. They are not truly repenting as they seek peace for their souls.

Take a man who has a wound caused by his sin and is troubled in his conscience. He has not walked uprightly according to the gospel, and things are not right between God and his soul. He now considers what is to be done. He knows what path he must take, and how he has been healed in the past. He must consider the promises of God. These promises must be applied to heal his sores and his troubled heart.

He comes to them, searches them out, and finds one or more of them whose literal expressions are directly suited to his condition. He says to himself, 'God speaks in this promise to me; I will draw from it a bandage sufficient to cover this wound.' He thus brings the Word to his condition and sets himself down in peace.

As we said before, the Lord is *near*, but is not *in* this wind! The work of the Spirit is not present. The Spirit alone can convince us of sin, righteousness and judgment. This is the work of the intelligent, rational soul, not of the Spirit.

It is possible for a regenerate man to act out of merely natural and rational principles, not out of his true spiritual life. He is acting merely upon the principle of conviction and illumination in his moral nature. The Holy Spirit is not moving on these waters.

Consider also the person who is troubled in conscience because he has fallen again into a sin which has troubled him before. No matter what the folly might be, even though it might be a small one, the fact that it is a recurring one makes it a deep wound, and it greatly troubles his heart. In the trouble of his mind he finds the promise of Isaiah 55:7 that the Lord will have mercy, and will abundantly pardon. That is, He will multiply or add to pardon, or He will do it again and again. Also Hosea 14:4, 'I will heal their apostasy; I will love them freely.' This man considers these great promises, and on this basis he grants peace to himself, whether the Spirit of God makes the application or not, or whether his application of the text is consistent with the intent of the author.

He does not consider whether it is indeed God who is speaking peace. He does not wait upon God, who yet may be hiding His face. God may see the poor creature stealing peace and running away with it, and knowing that the time will come when He will have to deal with him again over this very question. The man will have to realize that it is vain to take one step forward, unless it is God who is leading him by the hand.

A number of questions may arise because of what I have been saying. Let us consider one:

'Since this application of the Word to our hearts seems consistent with the usual path which the Holy Spirit also leads us in, to heal our wounds and quieten our hearts, how shall we know when we are going alone, and when the Spirit also leads us?'

Answer 1: If anyone is in error concerning this, God will speedily let him know it. We have this promise: 'He leads the humble in what is right, and teaches the humble His way' (*Psa.* 25:9). The Lord will not always let you err. He will, I say, not allow your nakedness to be covered with fig leaves. He will take them away, together with all the peace you have from trusting in them, and will not let you settle in this condition. You will quickly know your wound is not healed. The peace you obtain in this way will not last long. For a time the mind may be overpowered with its own convictions, so that there is nothing for any disquiet to fix upon; but after a little while such reasonings will grow cold, and vanish before the face of the first temptation that again arises to test you! But,

Answer 2: This course is commonly taken without waiting. Waiting is the grace and particular action of faith, which God calls us to when we are in such a condition. I know God sometimes comes upon a soul instantly, in a moment, as it were, wounding and healing the soul. So it was in the case of David, when he cut the hem of Saul's garment. But ordinarily, in such a case, God calls for waiting and labouring, attending in prayer as the eye of a servant rests upon his master. So says the prophet Isaiah (8:17): 'I will wait for the LORD, who is hiding his face from the house of Jacob.'

God will have his children lie a while at His door, when they have run from His house, and not instantly rush in upon Him; unless He takes them by the hand and pulls them in because they are so ashamed that they dare not come to Him. Now, self-healers, or men that speak peace to themselves, are commonly hasty. They will not wait a while. They do not wait for God to speak, but rush on seeking immediate healing.

Answer 3: Such a course, though it may quiet the conscience, the mind, and the reasonings of the soul, does not sweeten the heart with rest and gracious contentment. It is like the answer that Elisha gave Naaman, 'Go in peace' (*2 Kings* 5:19). It quieted his mind, but I question greatly whether it sweetened his heart, or gave him any joy in believing, other than the natural joy that was stirred in him because of his healing. 'Do not My words do good?' says the LORD (*Mic.* 2:7). When God speaks, there is not only truth in His words, there is healing. He not only addresses the convictions of our heart and our guilt, He brings that which is sweet, good, and desirable to our will and affections. By these blessings He returns our soul to rest (*Psa.* 116:7).

Answer 4: What is worst of all is that this course does not change the life. It does not heal the evil nor cure the disorder. When God speaks peace, He guides and keeps the soul so that it does not turn again to folly. When we speak peace to ourselves, the heart is not taken away from the evil; no, it is the quickest way to lead a soul into the habit of backsliding. When you seek to heal yourself, you find yourself prone to go back again, instead of being utterly weaned from your sin. This is a clear indication that you have sought to heal your own soul and that Jesus Christ and His Spirit were not there. Often the natural man, having done his own work of healing, will soon be ready to seek for a new wound! When God speaks peace, there comes along with it so much sweetness, and such a discovery of His love, that there is a strong inclination and desire to deal perversely no more!

Rule 3: Speaking peace to ourselves can be detected by the fact that we do it superficially. Jeremiah the prophet complains of some teachers: 'They have healed the wound of my people lightly' (*Jer.* 6:14).

This is the way it is with some persons. They make the healing of their wounds an insignificant work. A look and a glance of faith to the promise, and that does it, and so the matter is ended! Hebrews tells us that 'the word preached did not profit' some, because it was 'not mixed with faith' in them (*Heb.* 4:2, AV).

A mere look to the word of mercy in the promise is not enough, but it must be mingled with faith. Our faith allows us to enter into the heart of the promise, and then it does good to our souls!

Suppose you had a wound on your conscience which caused you weakness and unrest, and now you find yourself free from its guilt; I ask, how did you get free? 'I looked to the promises of pardon and healing, and I found peace!' Yes, but perhaps you were in too much of a hurry! You sought peace outwardly, but you did not feed upon the promise and mix it with your faith, so that it might diffuse all its virtues into your soul. You only dealt with your condition superficially. You will find your wound, before long, breaking out again. Then you will know that you are not cured.

Rule 4: A person also speaks peace to himself when he is concerned about one sin, while at the same time there is another evil of no less importance lying upon his spirit, about which he has had no dealings with God. Such a person cries, 'Peace', when there is none.

For example, suppose a man has neglected a duty again and again which he rightly should have fulfilled. His conscience is perplexed, his soul is wounded, and he has no rest in his bones by reason of his sin. He applies himself for healing and he finds peace.

Yet, at the same time, perhaps, worldliness, or pride, or some other folly, by which the Holy Spirit of God is exceedingly grieved, lies in the bosom of that man, and these things do not disturb him, nor he them! Let not that man think that any of the peace he experiences is from God. It can only be well with men, when they have an equal respect for all of God's commandments. God will justify us from our sins, but He will not justify the least sin in us. He is a God 'of purer eyes than to see evil and cannot look at wrong' (*Hab.* 1:13).

Rule 5: When men speak peace to themselves, it is seldom the case that God at the same time speaks humiliation to their souls. But God's peace is humbling peace. It is melting peace. So, in the case of David (*Psa.* 51:1), there was never such deep humiliation as when Nathan came and brought to him the tidings of his pardon.

But you will say, 'When may we take the comfort of a promise as our own, in relation to some particular wound, for the quieting of our heart?'

First, in general, whenever God speaks the promise, whether sooner or later, we may claim it! God may do it in the very instant of the sin itself with such irresistible power that the soul clearly knows God is in it. Sometimes He will make us wait longer. But, when He speaks, whether it is sooner or later, whether when we are sinning or when we are repenting, we may trust His pardon. In our communion with God, He is most troubled by our unbelieving fears. These keep us from receiving the strong comfort He is so willing to give us!

But you will reply, 'We are back where we started. When God speaks, we must receive it; that is true, but how shall we know *when it is He who speaks?*'

I answer, first, I wish it were true in practice that we could all receive peace when we are convinced that God is speaking it to us, and that it is our duty to receive it. But unbelief frequently prevents this.

But, secondly, there is, if I may put it in this way, a secret instinct in faith, whereby it knows the voice of Christ when He truly speaks. As the babe leaped in the womb when the blessed Virgin came to Elisabeth, faith leaps in the heart when Christ indeed draws near. 'My sheep', said Christ, 'hear my voice' (*John* 10:27). 'They know My voice; they are used to the sound of it.' They know when His lips are opened to them and are full of grace.

In the Song of Solomon (5:2), the bride knows the voice of her beloved. As soon as he speaks she cries, 'It is the voice of my beloved!' She knew his voice and was so accustomed to communion with him that she instantly recognized him. So will you know the voice of Christ. If you exercise yourselves to know and have fellowship with Him, you will easily discern between His voice and the voice of a stranger.

Note this: When he speaks, he speaks as no man has ever spoken. He speaks with power. He will in one way or another make your heart burn within you (*Luke* 24). When He puts his hand to the latch (*Song of Sol.* 5:4), His Spirit will seize your heart!

Each one who has exercised himself to discern good and evil, and is increasing in judgment, experience, and observation to recognize Christ's voice, and the operations of His Holy Spirit, is the best equipped to judge for himself when God is indeed speaking.

But secondly, as to when we may take the comfort of a promise to ourselves: If the Word of the Lord does good to your soul, He is the one who speaks it. If it humbles you and cleanses you, it is fulfilling the purpose for which it was given to you, namely to endear, to cleanse, to melt and bind to obedience, and to self-emptiness, and so on.

Without a right consideration of this, sin will have a great advantage, and tend to the hardening of the heart!

14

The Work of Christ and the Power of the Spirit

The things that we have considered so far have been in preparation for the work of mortification, rather than to effect it. They are necessary to prepare the heart, and without them this work cannot be accomplished. The directions for the work itself are only two.

Direction 1:
Set your faith upon Christ for the killing of your sin. His blood is the great sovereign remedy for sin-sick souls. Live in the light of Christ's great work, and you will die a conqueror. You will, through the good providence of God, live to see your lust dead at your feet.

But you will say, 'How can we look by faith to Christ for this great purpose?'

Consider several ways:

1. *By faith fill your heart with a right consideration of the provision that God has made in the work of Christ for the mortification of your sins.* By faith ponder this, that though you are in no way able to conquer your own disordered state, and though you are weary of fighting it, and though you are ready to faint, there is enough in Jesus Christ to give you relief! 'I can do all things through him who strengthens me' (*Phil.* 4:13).

This helped the prodigal when he was about to faint, that there was enough bread in his father's house. Even though he was a great distance from home it relieved him and strengthened him that at home he would find help. In your greatest distress and anguish, consider the fullness of grace, all the riches and treasures of strength, might, and help that are laid up in Christ for our support. 'And from his fullness we have all received, grace upon grace' (*John* 1:16). 'For in him all the fullness of God was pleased to dwell' (*Col.* 1:19).

Let these great truths abide in your mind. Consider that He is exalted and made a 'Leader and Saviour, to give repentance to Israel' (*Acts* 5:31). If He came to give repentance, then also mortification! True repentance must include mortification. Christ tells us that we obtain purging grace by abiding in him (*John* 15:3). To trust in the fullness we have in Christ for our supply is an important part of our abiding in Christ. Both our introduction into Christ and our abiding in Christ are by faith (*Rom.* 11:19–20).

Therefore, let your soul, by faith, dwell on such thoughts as these:

I am a poor, weak creature; unstable as water, and I cannot excel. This corruption is too hard for me, and is the doorway to the ruin of my soul. I do not know what to do.

My soul has become parched ground, and a habitation of dragons. I have made promises and broken them. I have made vows, but I did not keep them. Many times I have been persuaded that I have gained the victory, and that I should be delivered, but I was deceived. Now I plainly see that without some great help and assistance, I will perish and be forced to abandon God.

But yet, though this is my state and condition, I will lift up my hands that hang down, and strengthen my feeble knees, for, behold, the Lord Jesus Christ has all the fullness of grace in His heart, and all the fullness of power in His hand. He is able to slay all of these enemies. There is sufficient provision in Him for my relief and assistance. He can take my drooping, dying soul and make me more than a conqueror (*Rom.* 8:37)!

'Why do you say, O Jacob, and speak, O Israel, "My way is hidden from the LORD, and my right is disregarded by my God"? Have you not known? Have you not heard? The LORD is the everlasting God, the Creator of the ends of the earth. He does not faint or grow weary; his understanding is unsearchable. He gives power to the faint, and to him who has no might he increases strength. Even youths shall faint and grow weary, and young men shall fall exhausted; but they who wait for the LORD shall renew their strength; they shall mount up with wings like eagles; they shall run and not be weary; they shall walk and not faint' (*Isa.* 40:27–31).

He can make the dry, parched ground of my soul to become a pool, and my thirsty, barren heart as springs of water. Yes, He can make this habitation of dragons, this heart, which is so full of abominable lusts and fiery temptations, to be a place of bounty and fruitfulness unto Himself (see *Isa.* 35:7)!

God strengthened Paul under his temptation, with the sufficiency of His grace: 'My grace is sufficient for you' (*2 Cor.* 12:9). Paul was not immediately released from his trial, yet the sufficiency of God's grace sustained him.

I say, then, we must by faith consider the supply and fullness that we have in Christ Jesus, and how He can at any time give strength and deliverance. If you do not immediately find success in your battle, you will at least be secure in your chariot, and you will not flee from the field while the conflict continues. You will be kept from utter discouragement and lying down in unbelief, and from turning aside to false means and remedies that cannot help you in the end. The effectiveness of this consideration will be found only in actual practice.

2. Secondly, *raise up your heart in faith with an expectation of relief from Christ.* Relief from Christ in this case is like the prophet's vision:

'For still the vision awaits its appointed time;
It hastens to the end – it will not lie.
If it seems slow, wait for it;
It will surely come; it will not delay' (*Hab.* 2:3).

Though it seems a long time to you while you are in your trouble and perplexity, yet the victory shall surely come in the appointed time from the Lord Jesus Christ. When it comes, that will be the best season for its accomplishment. If you can raise up your heart to a settled expectation of help from Jesus Christ, keeping your eyes upon Him, 'as the eyes of servants look to the hand of their master' (*Psa.* 123:2), when they expect to receive something from him, your soul will be satisfied, and He will assuredly deliver you. He will slay your lusts, and your latter end will be peace. Look for it from His hand with an expectation of when and how He might do it. 'If ye will not believe, surely ye shall not be established' (*Isa.* 7:9, AV).

But you might say; 'What ground do I have to build such an expectation on, so as not to be deceived?'

Your need has directed you into this course for help. You will be relieved and saved this way, or not at all. Where else can you go? There are in the Lord Jesus innumerable reasons to encourage and engage you to this expectation.

It is necessary to remember, as I have pointed out before, that mortification is the work of faith and of believers only. 'Apart from me', said Christ, 'you can do nothing' (*John* 15:5). He was speaking here about purging the heart from sin. Mortification of any sin must be through a supply of grace. We cannot do it by ourselves.

It is in Christ that all fullness dwells (*Col.* 1:19) and it is from His fullness that we are to receive, and grace for grace (*John* 1:16).

Christ is the fountain from which the new man must draw the influences of life and strength, or he will decay every day. If we are 'strengthened with power . . . in [our] inner being', it is by Christ's 'dwelling in [our] hearts through faith' (*Eph.* 3:16–17).

That this work is not to be done without the Holy Spirit we have already considered. You might ask: 'Whence, then, do we expect the Spirit? From whom do we look for Him? Who has promised Him to us? Who has secured His aid for us?' Is not the answer to all these questions, *Christ alone*?

Let this, then, be a fixed principle in your hearts. If you do not get help from Him, you will not find help from any one! Any other way or endeavour without Christ's help will be to no purpose. It will do you no good. Only Christ and the means appointed by Him will give you lasting help.

Let us consider two additional reasons for this expectation of relief:

i. *Consider His mercy, tenderness, and kindness as He represents us as our great High Priest at the right hand of God.* Certainly He pities you in your distress. He says, 'As one whom his mother comforts, so I will comfort you'

(*Isa.* 66:13). He has the tenderness of a mother to a nursing child. Also, 'He had to be made like his brothers in every respect, so that he might become a merciful and faithful high priest in the service of God, to make propitiation for the sins of the people. For because he himself has suffered when tempted, he is able to help those who are being tempted' (*Heb.* 2:17–18).

Did the sufferings and temptations of Christ add to His ability and power to help us? No. The ability here mentioned is His readiness and willingness to come to our aid against all opposition. He is able, having suffered and been tempted, to break through all reasons to the contrary, and to relieve poor tempted souls. Having suffered Himself, He is moved to help.

'For we do not have a high priest who is unable to sympathize with our weaknesses, but one who in every respect has been tempted as we are, yet without sin. Let us then with confidence draw near to the throne of grace, that we may receive mercy and find grace to help in time of need' (*Heb.* 4:15–16).

The exhortation of verse 16 is the very point I wish to make, namely, that we should expect relief from Christ in 'time of need'! Says the tried soul, 'This is what I long for, grace in time of need. I am ready to die, to perish, to be lost for ever, and iniquity will prevail against me, if help does not come.' The apostle tells us to expect this help and grace from Christ. Yes, but on what account? Because He is a faithful and merciful high priest! I shall be bold to say that this one thing of expecting relief from Christ, on the basis of His mercy as our high priest, will be a better and speedier means of destroying your lust and the disorder of your soul than all the most rigid efforts at self-mortification that the sons of men engage in. Yes, and let me add that no soul has ever perished by the power of any lust, sin, or corruption who could raise his soul by faith to expect such relief from Jesus Christ (*Isa.* 55:1–3; *Rev.* 3:18).

ii. *Consider also the faithfulness of Him who has promised.* Considering this great attribute will strengthen your expectation of His help. God has promised to send relief in our need. He will fulfil His word to the utmost. God compares His covenant with us to the order of the heavens. The sun, moon, and stars all have their ordained courses which do not change (*Jer.* 31:36). David said that he watched for help from God as one who watches for the morning (*Psa.* 130:6), something that will surely come at its appointed time. Your relief from Christ will be like this. It will come in its season, as the dew and rain upon the parched ground, for faithful is He who has promised.

Particular promises to this effect are innumerable; let your soul always be furnished with them, especially those that seem particularly appropriate to your condition.

There are two particular advantages that always attend this expectation of help from Jesus Christ:

a. *It engages the Lord to give a full and speedy assistance.* Nothing motivates the heart of a man to be useful and helpful to another more than when the other looks to him for help. The kindness, care, and promises of Christ encourage us to expect His help. Our rising to seek it in our time of need must greatly engage His heart to assist us. The Psalmist gives us this certain truth, that the Lord does not forsake those that seek Him (*Psa.* 9:10). When the heart learns to rest in God, the Lord will surely vindicate his confidence! He will never be as a supply of water that fails; nor has the Lord ever said to the seed of Jacob, 'Seek My face in vain.' If Christ is the fountain of our supply, He will not fail us.

b. *It encourages the heart to make diligent use of every means by which Christ may reveal Himself to the soul.* It therefore takes in all the help that graces and ordinances can give. When you expect help from a man, you use means to obtain what you are seeking. The beggar that expects alms will lie at the door or in the way of the one from whom he seeks help. The ways and means by which Christ usually communicates Himself are His ordinances. He that is seeking help from Christ should seek Him in these!

As our faith looks to Christ for help, it sets our hearts to work. It is not an idle, groundless hope. If there is any vigour, efficacy, and power in prayer or sacrament to help in mortifying sin, a man will assuredly be interested in it all, because of his expectation of help. On this account I would reduce all specific action by means of prayer, meditation, and the like, to the same head.

All these are of great use when they are based on this expectation of help from Christ and spring from this root, though they are only of use when this is their basis.

Now concerning this direction for the mortification of a prevailing disorder in the soul, you may have a thousand testimonials to its value. Who is there, among those who walk with God, who has not verified its use and success? I dare to leave the soul under this direction without adding any more. I would only mention some particulars relating to what has been said.

1. *Place your faith particularly upon the death, blood, and cross of Christ; that is, on Christ as crucified and slain.*

Mortification is based particularly upon the death of Christ. This is one of the main purposes of the death of Christ, and shall assuredly be accomplished by it. He died to destroy the works of the devil. Both our fallen nature, as a result of Satan's temptation in the Garden of Eden, and the strength of his continued suggestions in daily life, were destroyed by the work of Christ! He died to destroy it all.

He 'gave himself for us to redeem us from all lawlessness and to purify for himself a people for his own possession who are zealous for good works' (*Titus* 2:14).

This was His aim and intention in giving Himself for us. In this He will not fail! He died that we might be freed from the power of our sins, and be purified from all of our defiling lusts. This purpose of His cannot fail!

'Christ loved the church and gave himself up for her, that he might sanctify her, having cleansed her . . . so that he might present the church to himself in splendour, without spot or wrinkle or any such thing, that she might be holy and without blemish' (*Eph.* 5:25–27).

This, by the virtue of His death, will be accomplished in varying degrees. Our washing, purging, and cleansing is everywhere ascribed to His blood (*1 John* 1:7; *Heb.* 1:3; *Rev.* 1:5). His blood, being sprinkled on us, purifies 'our conscience from dead works to serve the living God' (*Heb.* 9:14). This is what we aim at. Of this we are in pursuit, that our consciences may be purged from dead works, that they may be rooted out, destroyed, and have no place in us any more. This shall certainly be brought about by the death of Christ. His virtue will go out to us for this purpose. All the supplies of the Spirit, and all the expressions of His grace and power come solely from this. Thus Paul says, 'How can we who died to sin still live in it?' (*Rom.* 6:2).

We are dead to sin by profession; dead to sin by obligation to be so; dead to sin by participation in His virtue and power for the killing of it; dead to sin by union and interest in Christ, through whom and by whom it is killed. How can we thus live in it? This Paul presses home by several considerations, all based upon the death of Christ in the following verses of Romans 6. He goes on: 'Do you not know that all of us who have been baptized into Christ Jesus were baptized into His death?' We have in baptism an evidence of our implanting into Christ. We

AT TIME OF ORDER AND ARE **NON-RETURNABLE**

OVED AND ON FILE).

AND NON-REFUNDABLE.

FINAL PRICING.

ED TO COMPLETE AN INSTALLATION WILL BE

YOUR INSTALLATION IN A TIMELY AND
RESPONSIBLE FOR ANCILLARY EXPENSE, i.e.:
IENCE, ETC......

mate, whether signing for his/her own
partnership, limited liability company or
yment of any and all sums to become due
for products and/or labor provided.

	3:53PM
Material:	290.55
Service:	0.00
Misc. Charges:	0.00
Sales Tax:	17.43
Misc. Tax:	0.00
QUOTE TOTAL:	**$307.98**

are baptized into Him. But into an interest in what are we baptized? Surely, 'his death', if indeed we are baptized into Christ in more than just the outward profession. What is the result?

'That, just as Christ was raised from the dead by the glory of the Father, we too might walk in newness of life . . . We know that our old self was crucified with him in order that the body of sin might be brought to nothing, so that we would no longer be enslaved to sin' (*Rom.* 6:4–6).

Our being baptized into the death of Christ means our being dead to sin and having our corruptions mortified. He was put to death for sin. He was raised up to glory, so that we might be raised up to grace and newness of life. The death of Christ crucified our old man, that the body of sin might be destroyed. Our being crucified *with* Him does not refer to *time*, but *causality*. His death was meritoriously the cause of our victory. By His death He secured the Holy Spirit for us to mortify sin. From His death comes virtue for our crucifying of the flesh. He was our Representative and Example. We shall surely be crucified to sin, as He was for our sin. This is what Paul means. In death, Christ destroyed the works of the devil, and secured the Holy Spirit for us, ensuring the destruction of sin, as to its reign in believers, that it should not obtain its end or its dominion.

2. *When you meditate upon the death of Christ, keep in mind the power available to us, and your desire to be conformed to Christ (Phil. 3:10; Col. 3:3; 1 Pet. 1:18–19).*

Let faith gaze upon Christ as He is set forth crucified and dying for us. Look upon Him under the weight of our sins, praying, bleeding, and dying (*1 Cor.* 15:3; *1 Pet.* 1:18–19; 5:1–2; *Col.* 1:13–14). Bring Him in that condition into your heart by faith. Apply His blood so shed to your corruptions. Do this daily.

Direction 2:

Finally, consider the part that the Holy Spirit plays in mortification and the effects that are particularly ascribed to Him.

In one word, this whole work, which I have described as our duty, is effected, carried on, and accomplished by the power of the Spirit in all its parts and all its degrees.

1. *He alone clearly and fully convinces the heart of the evil, guilt, and danger of the corruption, lust or sin that is to be mortified.* Without this conviction, or while this conviction is so weak that the heart can overcome it or put up with it, there will be no thorough progress made toward mortification. An unbelieving heart (which we all have in part) will compromise easily, unless it is overpowered by clear and powerful convictions.

This is the specific work of the Holy Spirit. He convicts of sin (*John* 16:8). He alone can do it. If the preaching of the Word joined with the reasonings of man were capable of bringing the conviction of sin, we would see much more conviction than we do. The preaching of the Word brings the truth that men are sinners and guilty before

God. It may communicate the nature of sin, and the fact that man is guilty. This light, however, is not powerful nor does it lay hold of the soul. Preaching and reasoning alone cannot cause the soul to feel these truths, and to produce a suitable response! There are wise and knowledgeable men, but devoid of the Spirit, who do not consider some things to be sin at all, but which are clearly the movings of lust. It is the Spirit alone that can do, and does do, this work.

This is the first work of the Spirit to bring about mortification. He convinces the soul of all its evil. He cuts off all of lust's pleadings, uncovers all of its deceits, stops all of its evasions, and answers its self-justifications. He makes the soul to confess the abomination of its sin, and to be cast down under the guilt of it. Unless this is done, all that follows is in vain.

2. *The Spirit alone reveals to us the fullness of Christ for our relief.* This consideration guards the heart from false ways, and from despair.

3. *The Spirit alone establishes the heart in the expectation of relief from Christ.* This is the great sovereign means of mortification, as we have seen.

4. *The Spirit alone brings the cross of Christ into our hearts with its sin-killing power.* By the Spirit we are baptized into the death of Christ.

5. *The Spirit is the Author and Finisher of our sanctification*. He gives new supplies and influences of grace for holiness and sanctification when our resolve to resist is weakened (*Eph*. 3:16–18).

6. *All of our soul's prayers to God in our need are supported by the Spirit*. From where do we find power, life, and vigour in prayer? Is it not from the Spirit? He is the 'Spirit of supplication' promised to those who look on Him 'whom they pierced' (*Zech*. 12:10). He enables us to pray with sighs and 'groanings too deep for words' (*Rom*. 8:26). This is surely the great way to prevail with God. This is how Paul dealt with his temptation: 'I pleaded with the Lord . . . that it should leave me' (*2 Cor*. 12:8). What the work of the Spirit in prayer is, and what we are to do that we may enjoy His help for that purpose, I have spoken of in another place.[1]

[1] See Owen's *Works*, vol. 4 (London: Banner of Truth, 1967), 'On the Work of the Holy Spirit in Prayer', pp. 235–350; and *The Spirit and the Church* (Edinburgh: Banner of Truth, 2002), 'Part 3: The Holy Spirit and Prayer', pp. 89–142.

Other John Owen titles in this series:

THE HOLY SPIRIT

'*Owen on the Holy Spirit*', as this work has been known to generations of Christians, is without question one of the truly great Christian books. Originally published in 1674 as *Pneumatologia, or A Discourse concerning the Holy Spirit,* it is a massive work, taking up 650 pages in the Banner of Truth edition of Owen's *Works* (Volume 3). This abridged version prepared by Dr R. J. K. Law will help modern readers to get to grips with Owen.

'An admirable effort at making this great 17th century Puritan theologian and teacher more accessible to the Christian reading public.'

New Life

ISBN 978 0 85151 698 1, 216 pp. Paperback

THE SPIRIT AND THE CHURCH

How do Christians come to the certainty that the Bible is the Word of God, and gain an understanding of his mind and will from it? How do they acquire the ability to pray and lead others in prayer? How are they comforted and supported in all the difficulties they meet? And how can the church be led, taught and guided aright, when Christ is not here on earth? According to Owen, the answer to all these questions is the same: *by the gracious and powerful work of the Holy Spirit.* This title brings together abridgements of four treatises in volume 4 of *The Works of John Owen.*

'We would urge readers to try this as an introduction to the ministry of John Owen . . . You really would not realize you were reading a Puritan—except for the freshness and helpfulness of the materia!'

Metropolitan Tabernacle Bookshop

ISBN 978 0 85151 822 0, 208 pp. Paperback

THE GLORY OF CHRIST

This abridgement shows John Owen at his richest and most mature as he expounds the heart of the gospel with biblical insight and understanding. He speaks to our own generation from his nearness to eternity and teaches us how to see Christ more clearly and serve him more faithfully.

'This is a book to warm the heart as well as instruct the mind.'

AUSTRALIAN PRESBYTERIAN

ISBN 978 0 85151 661 5, 184 pp. Paperback

COMMUNION WITH GOD

Owen believed that communion with God lay at the heart of the Christian life. He never lost the sense of amazement expressed by John: 'Our fellowship is with the Father and with his Son, Jesus Christ.'

'A delight to read . . . as [Owen] beautifully and personally applies Scripture.'

REFORMED THEOLOGICAL JOURNAL

ISBN 978 0 85151 607 3, 224 pp. Paperback

APOSTASY FROM THE GOSPEL

The idea that professing Christians may prove not to be true Christians is deeply disturbing, but this is not a reason to avoid the issue. This modernized abridgement of Owen's work makes its powerful teaching readily accessible to modern readers. It is a work which wounds in order to heal.

'A masterpiece of spiritual penetration and insight.'

FREE CHURCH MONTHLY RECORD

ISBN 978 0 85151 609 7, 184 pp. Paperback

For more information about our publications, or to order, please visit our website.

THE BANNER OF TRUTH TRUST

3 Murrayfield Road,   P O Box 621, Carlisle,
Edinburgh EH12 6EL   PA 17013,
UK   USA
www.banneroftruth.co.uk